THE JAGUAR CHALLENGE

KEN WELLS

OVERSEAS DISTRIBUTORS

VID BATEMAN LIMITED,
Golden Heights
-34 View Road, Glenfield,
Auckland 10

Motorbooks International
Publishers & Wholesalers Inc
Osceola, Wisconsin 54020, USA

Osceola,
Wisconsin 54020, USA

EDITIONS E.P.A.,
18 rue d'Issy,
92100 Boulogne-Billancourt, France

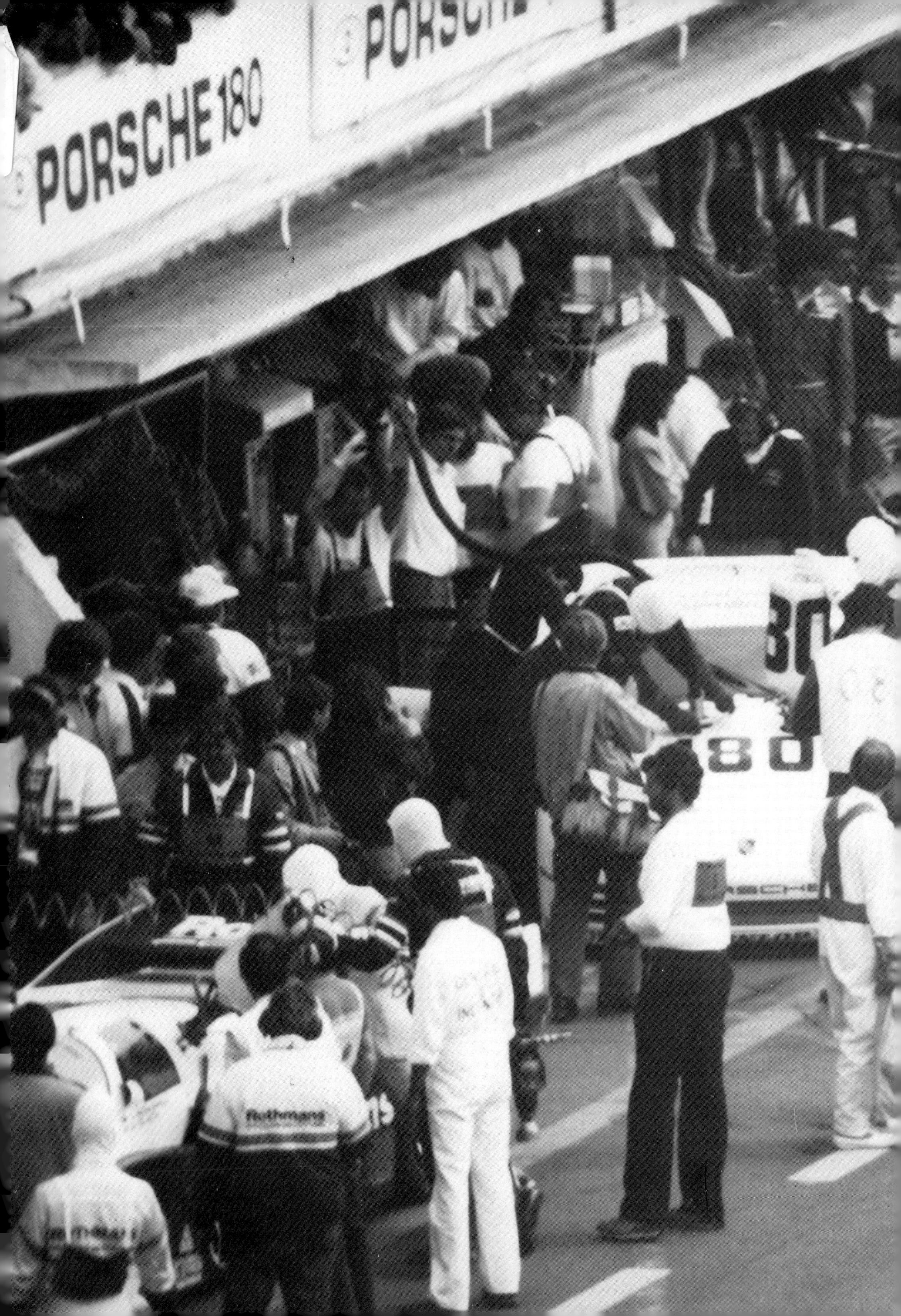

PORSCHE
PORSCHE 180
180
Rothmans

CONTENTS

Le Mans Retrospective	4
The Jaguar Decade	8
Jacky Ickx's Le Mans	13
Purple Phase	16
Purple Plaque	20
The Season so far	22
The Jaguar Challenge	26
The French Resistance	42
Car Comparison	49
Urd about Le Mans	50
Good Ol' Boys	54
Fitness and Fast Food	58
Attitudes and Alarums	58
New Technology	59
Sarthe Snippets	60
The French Challengers	63
The Race	72
Per Arnage ad Astra	98
Ford Fiesta	99
What Happened Next	100
Statistics	105

Published by:	Kimberley's Publishers, 4 Church Close, London, N20 0JU.
First Published:	December, 1986 ©Kewkar Racing and Kimberley's Publishers
Printed by:	The Lavenham Press Limited Lavenham, Suffolk CO10 9RN. England
Photographers:	David Cundy, Ken Wells
Additional material:	Gordon Dawkins, The National Motor Museum William Kimberley
Writers:	Ken Wells, David Cundy
Special thanks to:	M. Mordret of the A.C.O., Mr. McCubbin of Fuji, Alan Collins and Barry Bass Kevin Pilcher and Pete Woods Southend College of Technology notably Roger Elson and Steve Gibbs
Special Note:	Copies of most of the photographs herein - and many more - are available from: Kewkar Racing, 4 Highfield Rise, Althorne, Essex CM3 6DN, England. Please enclosed a stamped, addressed envelope with any enquiry.

ISBN 0 946132 39 9

LE MANS RETROSPECTIVE

Since the dawn of the motoring age, Le Mans and motor racing seem to have been synonymous with one another. For instance, on 9th October 1875, Amedee Bollee, a well known bell-maker of the city, made one of the first great pioneering runs of early motoring history from Le Mans to Paris aboard his steam brake *L'Obeissante*. Along his route Bollee ran into considerable trouble from local law enforcement officers receiving from them over 70 summonses. Fortunately for him they were all subsequently squashed. Although Bollee died long ago, *L'Obeissante* still survives in all her ancient splendour in the Conservatoire des Arts et Metiers in Paris.

When the first ever race was run under the title of Grand Prix, it was Le Mans which was selected from a great many contenders to stage the event. The Grand Prix took place on a 63½ mile long circuit to the east of the city on Tuesday and Wednesday, 26th and 27th June, 1906. On each of the two days, the competitors had to complete 6 laps of the circuit, with victory finally going to the Hungarian driver Ferenc Szisz on a monster Renault of some 12,986cc capacity. His average speed for the race was an astounding 61.3mph over roads that were little better than dirt tracks.

When the madness of the First World War was over, it was once again the Le Mans circuit which, in 1921, staged the first post-war Grand Prix. The race was won for the first time by an American car/driver combination, Jimmy Murphy driving a Duesenberg taking the chequered flag in front of two French Ballots of Ralph de Palma and Jules Goux. This victory did not go down at all well with Murphy's French hosts; they were in Queen Victoria's immortal words 'not amused'. It was to be over 40 years before another Grand Prix was won by an American driver in the cockpit of an American car, when Dan Gurney took his Eagle Gurney Weslake to victory in the 1967 Belgian Grand Prix at Spa.

In 1922 an historic meeting took place between Charles Faroux and Georges Durand where it was argued that for the man in the street to become interested in motor sport, a race should be inaugurated for production cars in normal road trim, and to make the race more interesting, it should be a true Grand Prix of endurance of over 24 hours. In Le Mans, the French had the ideal circuit, perfect for the purpose intended, as, for most of the year it consisted of normal roads used by everyday traffic. So the *24 Heures du Mans* was born with the first race taking place in 1923.

Altogether there have been 54 races run on a total of eight different circuits which have ranged in length from 8.364 miles to 10.726 miles, and although the circuit has been modified greatly, during these changes the basis of the circuit has always included Tetre Rouge, Hunaudieres, Arnage and possibly the most famous piece of race track anywhere in the world, the Mulsanne Straight.

It is the Bentley marque that epitomises prewar Le Mans. Barnato's Bentley has just regained the lead from the Stutz in the 1928 race. The Bentley covered a total of 1,677·247 miles, only 7·878 more than the Stutz.

Equally famous in its own way the Le Mans start was used from 1925 to 1969 when it was abandoned due to safety reasons. The fastest race lap ever recorded on any of the circuits was in 1971 when Jackie Oliver recorded a time of 3m18.4s in his Gulf Porsche 917 at an average speed of 151.86mph. The greatest distance ever covered by a car in the race was also in 1971 when the Helmut Marko/Gijs van Lennep Martini Racing Porsche 917 recorded a distance of 3315.203 miles, an average speed of 138.133mph. Officially the fastest time ever recorded through the speed trap at Hunauderies was set by the Joest Racing Porsche 956 of Klaus Ludwig in the 1985 race with a speed of some 231mph, but it is generally reckoned that Oliver in the Gulf Porsche 917 was probably touching 240-245mph at Hunauderies on his 1971 record lap.

Fastest lap ever recorded on any of the circuits was set by the German driver Hans Stuck in a works Rothmans Porsche 962 in practice for the 1985 race. Stuck swept round the circuit in 3m 14.8s, an average speed of 156.46mph.

In the 1927 race the Bentley of Davis/Benjafield recorded the greates ever winning distance when it beat the French Salmson of De Victor/Hasley by 217.8 miles. The bald facts do no justice to the true drama of the race which was a rea cliff-hanger to the very end. The entry consisted of 22 cars, three of which were Bentleys, one of which it was assumed by the fans would win the race. In those far of days when the starting flag was dropped the drivers sprinted across to their cars and immediately erected the hoods, after which

they commenced the race proper. The cars had to race with their hoods in the up position for 214 miles as a condition of the rules of the race, the sight reminiscent of 12 ships in full sail.

The race got off to a good start for the Bentley team as they took up a 1-2-3 formation at the head of the field. Unkind fates, however, took a hand in the race, and as daylight turned to dusk a major accident at the White House eliminated two of the Bentleys and all but wrecked the third. Davis, who was driving the third

Bentley at the time, extricated the car from the mess and drove it to the pits for repairs.

The damage to the Bentley was extensive: a front wing was askew and the car had no lights; the steering was damaged and the brakes were pulling sideways - hardly the condition in which to win a motor race. It was decided, however, that the car should continue. On re-entering the fray, the Bentley was some six laps behind the French Aries driven by Laly/Chassagne which was leading the race. The following morning brought a different story when a sharp eared mechanic on the Bentley team heard a non-standard note to the engine of the Aries. In spite of the state the Bentley was in, it was decided by the Bentley pit to force the pace and speed up the mobile wreck that claimed to be the number three Bentley. This they did to such good effect that, in the early afternoon of the second day, the Aries succumbed to engine failure. It then only remained for the Bentley to cruise home to the greatest winning margin ever recorded in the race, and another page in the history of the race.

The shortest race-winning distance was in 1966 when Chris Amon and Bruce McLaren in a Ford beat the sister car of Ken Miles and Denny Hulme by 20 metres, but this result was pre-arranged by the Ford management to be a dead-heat, (unfortunately it went wrong), so it cannot really qualify, leaving the 1969 result as the shortest race-winning distance ever recorded.

In that race the glorious Porsche 917 made its appearance with Rolf Stommelen leading in one of them for the first three hours of the race, after which his team

mates, Dick Attwood and Vic Elford in a sister 917 lead for a further 18 hours before clutch trouble put them out of the running. The battle for the lead was then well and truly joined as the Ickx/Oliver Ford GT40 and the Herrmann/Larrousse Porsche 908 fought tooth and nail to the finish. In the end the Ickx/Oliver GT40 just won the race by 120 metres. This victory was the first of a record six victories achieved by Ickx at Le Mans and was also the first time that the same car had won the race two years in succession.

The only other car to win for two consecutive years was the Joest Racing Porsche 956 when it crossed the finish line in first place in 1984 and 1985.

Le Mans has produced some of the truly great classics of motor racing history, races that have been filled with drama, tension and excitement, conversely it has also produced deadly boring affairs where the sooner the race was over the better. One race, however, produced the stuff that nightmares are made of when an accident to the Mercedes 300 SLR of Pierre Levegh caused the car to explode into the crowd killing Levegh himself and 80 other people in the worst tragedy motor racing has known.

Come next June, that famous old circuit at La Sarthe will once again re-echo to the sound of racing exhausts, excitement will rip through the air, tension will build up to that famous 4 o'clock start and the 55th *24 Heures du Mans* will take place. It is exciting, boring, tension filled, deadly dangerous for the drivers, tiring, all these and more, but is there any other race in the world quite like it? (DC)

Left: Bernard Rubin changes the plugs on No. 4, 4½-litre Bentley which, shared with Woolf Barnato, won the 1928 race at 69.11 mph. Below: The Ickx/Oliver GT40 that won The 1969 race by 120 metres.

THE JAGUAR DECADE

A few years ago a space probe was sent into the heavens with the hope of contacting other life forms somewhere this side of infinity. It contained details of our position in the cosmos and a variety of artifacts detailing the history of Mother Earth.

Imagine, if you will, that you had been asked to provide the names of two motor racing marques to epitomise each decade of the sport. Your choices for the thirties would rest between Alfa Romeo, Bugatti, Mercedes Benz and Auto Union. The seventies would see Porsche, Lotus and Ferrari as top contenders for the ride into immortality. The selection for the fifties, I humbly suggest, would probably fall on Jaguar and Mercedes.

The perplexities of choosing two such time travellers for each decade would be multiplied if the projectile's payload were halved and your options limited to a single name! How could you choose between the vastly differing disciplines of motor sport? What, if any, is the ratio for success with a Grand Prix racer or a sports car? Today, is a McLaren MP4/2 better than a Porsche 956/962?

With the recent return of the factory blessed efforts, Jaguar and Mercedes are now back in top line sport together for the first time in 30 years. So now is an ideal time to review their exploits; to decide who would get the single place for the fifties on the spaceship of destiny. Grand Prix racing was the exclusive prerogative of the Germans - winning nine of the 12 races they entered during 1954/55, thus claiming two drivers (Fangio) and two constructors titles - while Jaguar limited their single seater efforts to 'Monzanapolis' challenges. They did, however, clash in sports cars, with many wins for both in races around the world. To help in your deliberations, we highlight their respective records at the greatest, most prestigious, of all these events - *Le Vingt-Quatre Heures du Mans.*

After the initial, unsuccessful, foray in 1950, the 120Cs returned a year later with Stirling Moss, in his first Le Mans, leading a Coventry 1-2-3 by sunset. But, as ever, he was out of luck and victory went to the sister car crewed by Whitehead and Walker.

For 1952 the three British Racing Green machines faced the trio of silver 300SL coupes as reigning champions and hot favourites to repeat their success. Sadly it was all to go wrong from the start for the British team when they suffered overheating problems in practice which repeated itself early in the race. Despite being amongst the leaders at the start, all gradually fell back and were out by the fourth hour - all their problems attributable to the overheating dramas.

Meantime the three German cars were all running well up the field until one suffered terminal dynamo trouble. When the Gordini of Behra aand Manzon retired at about half distance the remaining two Mercedes were then able to close ranks behind the Talbot-Lago of Levegh and Marchand.

It was in 1954 that Jaguar entered the D-type for the first time.
(National Motor Museum)

The curious thing about the Talbot-Lago was that Marchand had yet to drive the car as Pierre Levegh attempted to score a unique, single-handed, victory. Unfortunately he damaged the engine with only an hour to go and a dramatic win evaporated. This left the Mercedes with a fortuitous victory that even their legendary team manager, Alfred Neubauer, had not anticipated.

For 1953 Jaguar reverted to their '51 bodywork, so eliminating the cause of the overheating problem of the previous year. It was the first year of the Manufacturers' Championship so Le Mans saw a magnificent entry spoiled only by the absence of Mercedes who were taking a sabbatical in preparation for their latter assaults. Once Jaguar had seen off the early challenge of a couple of Alfas and the more determined efforts of the Ascari/Villoresi Ferrari, it was left to the leading Cunningham to claim third place behind the C-types of Rolt/Hamilton and Moss/Walker with the third 'cat' just behind the C-5R. The 1-2-4 result was a splendid way to allay the ghost of '52 - even a private C-type claimed ninth.

Mercedes were still not back for '54 but Jaguar turned up with three of the new D-types and there was a Belgian entered C for good measure. The race turned out to be a battle between the three Ferrari 375 'Plus' models and the Jaguars. The extra power of the five litre Italian engines enabled them to stay ahead of the more nimble 3442cc Jaguars despite the almost constant rain, but the British marque battled on gamely. Both teams lost a car early on, then another, so it was left by sunrise to be a straight fight between the scarlet of Gonzales and Trintignant and the British Racing Green of Rolt and Hamilton. The C-type was an encouraging fourth, splitting a pair of Cunninghams - the only other marque that was remotely competitive for outright honours. The Ferrari had a comfortable margin over the Jaguar until about two hours from the end when a long pit stop reduced the deficit from 10 to three minutes. This was further reduced by an inspired last stint by Duncan Hamilton so that with just half an hour to go the Big Cat was but 86 seconds behind. Alas, the sun appeared to dry out the track and the Jaguar got no closer. By flagfall he

was but two and a half miles behind - a splendid effort.

1955: Mercedes returned to the Sarthe circuit having swept all before them in the Grand Prix arena. The Germans had three superb 300 SLRs for Fangio/Moss, Kling/Simon while Fitch was paired with '52 hero Levegh. Pitted against them were a team of Ferraris and no less than five D-types. Castelloti and Marzotto led initially in their 121 LM before falling back to eventual early retirement so leaving the Fangio car to fight for the lead with the D of Hawthorn and Bueb. As Hawthorn came around to make his first pit stop after about 2½ hours racing, for some still unexplained reason, he decided to overtake Macklin's Austin-Healey before pitting. The driver had to take dramatic action to avoid the D hitting its bows, but only succeeded in swerving into the path of the following Levegh. The Mercedes cannoned into the barrier and broke up under impact killing the driver and 80 spectators. It was, and remains, the most horrific accident in the history of motor sport. The Mercedes and the Jaguar continued to battle for the lead while the

The D-type Jaguar which paraded before the 1986 race bears the legendary 774 RW plate of the '55 winner (KW).

second surviving silver car gradually made its way up the leader board after early problems. At 2am the Stuttgart team was withdrawn upon instructions from the board of directors, as a mark of respect to the disaster victims. This gave the Jaguars a 1-2 lead with the Hawthorn/Bueb car being followed by the Rolt/Hamilton version, with another, driven by Swaters and Claes running fifth behind an Aston Martin and a Maserati. Just after dawn on Sunday the second placed car expired with gearbox problems as did the Maserati, thus allowing the Belgian driven D into third place. These positions were maintained to the end, but it was a joyless victory for Hawthorn and Bueb.

New safety features heralded the 1956 race in an attempt to avoid a repetition of the '55 disaster. Mercedes had withdrawn from official competition and their only representative was a private 300 SL for Metternich and Einsiedel, but it was never to feature and retired with engine problems before nightfall.

The entry list was dominated by a multitude of Ferraris and no less than six Jaguars - five D-types and a remarkable XK140 for Walshaw and Bolton. The race started badly for the Coventry cars when Paul Frere crashed on the second lap and Jack Fairman's works entry was eliminated in the ensuing chaos. Two Jags out after only five minutes! The Hawthorn/Bueb car was an early pit visitor and its long delay to rectify fuel problems left it way down the leader board.

Up front, the Ecurie Ecosse D of Sanderson and Flockhart staged a magnificent battle with the DB3S of Moss/Collins with Ferrari unable to offer any challenge. The XK140 was disqualified with only four hours to go due to some re-fuelling irregularities while in 11th place.

By then the lead Jaguar had pulled clear of the Aston Martin and the Belgian D held fourth behind the surviving Ferrari. The final works Jaguar of the '55 winners overcame its early dramas to salvage sixth place, but all the accolades went to the two

privateers - particularly for the car in Scottish blue.

The next year, 1957, was one the Italians were determined to win, no less than 15 examples from Maserati and Ferrari combined. There were no works cars from Jaguar - the British manufacturer having withdrawn - but there were still five private D's to challenge the might of Italy.

Initially the Jaguars were left in the wake of the mighty red cars, but the pace of the competition between the rivals soon brought about the first of a spate of retirements. Flockhart/Bueb got to the front of the queue after three hours. By half distance, with more calamities for the Italians, the D-types filled the first four places while the other was already recovering from previous problems. It was over as a contest by then and only the final finishing order between the various Jaguars had to be resolved, the long time leaders finally getting the chequered flag well ahead of Lawrence and '56 winner Sanderson. The marque finally claimed 1-

The Hawthorn/Bueb D-type in the 1956 race. (National Motor Museum)

2-3-4-6, the fifth placed Ferrari denying a perfect result for Coventry. A stupendous victory!

Five D-types were entered again in '58 plus a couple of Jaguar-engined Listers, all of which had new short stroke engines for this year. Both the Ecurie Ecosse cars were eliminated with piston problems after the start, then the Charles/Young example crashed so there were three out within three hours and those were soon followed by a Lister suffering from oil pressure problems.

Up front two Ferraris battled with the Aston Martin of Brooks/Trintignant and the D of Hamilton and Bueb was putting up an excellent show - even leading briefly around midnight, but mainly running behind the 250TR of Gendebien and Phil Hill. The other remaining D had never shown and crashed out of the race before darkness set in so leaving the Jaguar challenge to the front running D and the Lister car of Halford and Naylor, which was running in the top 10 for many hours.

Unfortunately it was all to go sour within the last few hours when, first, the Lister dropped to 15th and Hamilton crashed at Arnage so handing an easy win to Ferrari with the private DB3S of the Whitehead brothers second. It was such an anti-climax after the previous years' successes and the death of 'Mary' at Tertre Rouge on Saturday night was the final straw.

The final race of the fifties saw one D-type for Ireland and Gregory plus two Listers and a Tojeiro example. Sadly none were to finish although most were amongst the front runners at some time during the early stages. The D broke a conrod after six hours while in second place behind eventual winners Salvadori and Shelby in their DBR1 whose sister car followed it home ahead of a gaggle of Ferraris.

Aston Martin, so often the poor Le Mans relation of Jaguar, at last achieved a well deserved victory to come out of the shadows of their illustrious fellow countrymen.

The fifties may have ended in disappointment for Jaguar, but their legend had been established beyond doubt and their name remains synonymous with the ultimate achievements at the Sarthe. Mercedes, on the other hand, have 1952 as their sole entry into the record books for this classic event.

The yardstick for the eighties has been the Porsche 956/962, but one wonders as to the possibilities of the new challengers from Jaguar and Mercedes emulating their illustrious predecessors. There is still time left for them to book their space on the rocket-ship to infinite immortality .... (KW)

In 1957 Jaguars scored a 1–2–3–4–6 result with the Flockhart/Bueb car (below) the last Jaguar to win at the Sarthe circuit in a 24 hour race. (National Motor Museum)

JACKY ICKX'S LE MANS

What was Jacky Ickx's best Le Mans race? With his retirement, the Sarthe supremo has left a question that could have enthusiasts arguing for a full 24 hours! Was it the first win, the famous sprint finish of '69? Or the dramatic victory of '77 after switching to another car? Maybe you would vote for the exciting second place of '83 or the epic charge for Ferrari in 1973? To choose one above the rest is like trying to classify a Beethoven symphony ahead of a Puccini opera, a Rembrandt instead of a Renoir. Each, like the majority of the Belgian maestro's 15 Le Mans starts, is a masterpiece in its own right, but it's nice thinking about it.....

It was in 1966 that the precocious 21 year old debuted at Le Mans. New rules and categories also made it the start of a new era for the *Vingt-Quatre Heures*. The new dawn heralded a new star. Jacky Ickx has seen many a new dawn at Le Mans since then and been the brightest light at many of them. The following paragraphs are intended as brief resumes of all the races of the last 20 years - the Ickx era - and highlight the part played by the walking epitome of Le Mans in their outcome. It is not just a story of 15 starts, six wins and four fastest laps. Often in the career of great men it is not only what they do but also what they do not do that makes the story complete. Jacky Ickx is no exception. Read on and decide for yourself: what was Jacky Ickx's best Le Mans race?

1966: Essex Wire Ford GT40 - DNF

Jochen Neerspach was Ickx's partner in the 4.7 litre machine. It was running well and in the top 10, like its sister car of Scott and Revson, when the engine broke in the early hours of Sunday morning. Meanwhile the Ford steamroller thundered on with the 7 litre monsters coming home 1-2-3 ahead of a quartet of 906s. Top place went to the antipodean pairing of McLaren and Amon who, after a stage-managed finish, were given the verdict over Hulme and Miles. The works Ferraris had long since packed up and gone home, humiliated, their challenge limited to a short, valiant effort by the Rodriguez/Ginther P3.

1967: JW Ford Mirage - DNF

John Wyer's much modified GT40-based car was shared with that amiable Aussie, Brian 'Yogi' Muir. Alas, the car never featured and expired, much to everyone's relief, after about three hours when a conrod broke. The sister vehicle of David Piper and Dick Thompson lasted little longer before being terminally afflicted with similar problems. Gurney and Foyt brought the Ford Mk IV to a star-spangled victory with another Mk IV fourth. They sandwiched the factory P4s of Scarfiotti/Parkes and Mairesse/'Beurlys' who were never in a position to break the American Dream.

1968: JW Gulf Ford GT40 - Did Not Enter

Civil unrest in France, highlighted by a summer of student riots, meant the race was postponed until late September. Just one week prior to the 24 Hours, the Ferrari Formula One driver crashed at the Canadian Grand Prix thereby breaking a leg. Ironically, Ickx's intended team mate, Brian Redman, was already *hors de combat* with a broken arm. Thus Pedro Rodriguez and Lucien Bianchi found themselves paired together and, by sunset, in the lead of the race. The 'Ickx' car then had an unchallenged run to the finish, ahead of two Porsches and three Alfa Romeos. Now, if the race had been run on its original date....

1969: JW Gulf Ford GT40 - FIRST

Any disappointment lingering from '68 was dispelled in the best possible way. Trailing the two leading Porsches with less than three hours to go, the Gulf car was ideally placed to capitalise on their demise. A classic battle then ensued with the 908 of Hermann and Larrousse, the lead forever changing. The Belgian finally outfoxed the wily German veteran at the exit from Mulsanne Corner on the last lap to snatch a dramatic victory for himself and Jackie Oliver. The official winning distance of 132 yards being the closest racing finish in the event's history. The Jacky Ickx/Le Mans legend was born.

A footnote to such an exciting finish occured at the very start - the last traditional Le Mans start. While most of his rivals sprinted to their machines and were quickly gone, the cool Belgian strolled to car number 6, methodically fastened his seatbelts and joined the rear of the fray. It is reckoned that when he left the pitlane the leaders, including the Hermann/Larrousse Porsche, were already at Tertre Rouge - more than a mile ahead. How fortunate that he had not stopped to re-tighten his shoelaces!

1970: Ferrari 512S - DNF

The wettest post-war Le Mans provided Porsche's first victory, the 917K driven by Richard Attwood and Hans Hermann - the latter getting ample revenge for his narrow defeat the previous year by promptly announcing his retirement! The Ickx/Peter Schetty car was the only opposition to stay with the 917s in the early stages and gradually made its way up to second place by midnight as the Porsches hit trouble. Two hours later the leader, driven by Siffert and Redman, also expired. At virtually the same time and so within sight of the race lead, Ickx crashed the Ferrari at the Ford chicane. Sadly, a marshall was fatally injured in the incident.

1971 : DID NOT ENTER

The sun returned for 1971 but the factory Ferraris didn't - hence no Jacky Ickx. Porsche won again, courtesy of Marko and Van Lennep, with the private Ferraris well beaten by the new, emerging force at the Sarthe. Attwood and Muller were second in another 917.

1972 : Ferrari 312P - DID NOT ENTER

Matra had an early scare when their fourth car suffered piston failure after only one hour. Nevertheless the remaining cars held a dominant 1-2-3 until shortly before the end when the last of the trio succumbed to gearbox troubles. A Porsche 908 thus salvaged third place. The celebrations were marred by the death of Jo Bonnier whose Lola left the track on Sunday morning. Where was Jacky Ickx? Armed with a 312P the Belgian had set a stunning time at the traditional Test Day in April. Two weeks before the big event the Ferrari management decided that the engine, designed for Six Hours/1000 Kms, would be unable to withstand the rigours of such a marathon. Ickx was left without a drive. Veni, vidi vamoos?

1973 : Ferrari 312P/B - DNF

Ironically it was with much the same car and engine as denied him the year before, that the Ferrari team leader appeared with in '73. Partnered by Redman - five years after their 'lost weekend' - each of the Scuderia team cars led for a period. Gradually the Ickx/Redman and Pescarolo/Larrousse (Matra) machines pulled clear to commence an epic battle for the latter part of the race. Both had long delays for various reasons but so great was their dominance that nobody else was able to take advantage of their problems. With less than two hours to go the Matra led by about one lap with the Ferrari vainly trying to get on terms with it. Just as the crowd warmed to the prospect of another close

13

finish it was all over. With only half an hour to go Ickx pitted with engine failure and the Ferrari was pushed away into retirement. The crowds gave the Belgian a superb reception for a valiant effort. Honours once again went to La Belle France.

1974 : DID NOT ENTER
Ickx had split, somewhat acrimoniously, from Ferrari and his sportscar drives for the season were restricted to some 'guest' appearances - including a win at Spa for Matra - but nothing for Le Mans. The 24-Hours provided a third successive win for Matra and Henri Pescarolo. Second place went to the surprisingly competitive Porsche Carrera Turbo of Muller and Van Lennep in an otherwise uninspiring race.

1975 : JW Gulf Mirage DFV - FIRST
The global fuel crisis inspired the organisers to devise what amounted to a consumption formula (Group C, *deja vu* ?) and they were instantly banned from the World Championship! This, in turn, meant the subsequent withdrawal of the works teams from Matra, Alfa Romeo and Ferrari. The new partnership of Ickx and Bell led, virtually untroubled, for most of the race. Then, a couple of hours from home the exhaust had to be replaced. While the Mirage was being worked on the Lafosse/Chasseuil Ligier JS2 got ever closer. The French team were within one lap when the Gulf car roared back onto the track to secure a popular win. The Ickx/Bell association was consecrated in champagne!

1976 : Martini Porsche 936 - FIRST
Some more rule changes meant a wider variety of cars than before to challenge for the ultimate test. Ickx was back, this time accompanied by former winner Gijs Van Lennep. Much like the previous year, the Ickx car drove into a virtually unassailable lead only to be severely delayed because of a damaged exhaust within sight of the finish. This time the opposition were not within sufficient striking distance to threaten. Lafosse claimed second again, this time in a Mirage and alongside Migault. The Lola of Craft/de Cadenet was a splendid third. The Mulsanne claimed another victim when Andre Haller crashed his Datsun 260Z.

1977 : Martini Porsche 936 - FIRST
Jacky Ickx scored his third consecutive victory - but his car retired after three hours! Originally teamed with Pescarolo, the leading works car was eliminated when the Frenchman over-revved the engine. Ickx was hastily drafted into the sister car,

alongside Hurley Heywood and Jurgen Barth, which was then lying in fifteenth place after fuel pump problems. It was the start of a brilliant, inspired drive. By half time, mainly due to Ickx's pace, they were up to second place behind Jabouille and Bell who had led virtually from the start. Six hours later the seemingly uncatchable Alpine blew up and Ickx, once again, led Le Mans. All that magnificent effort looked like paying off. Suddenly, an hour from the end, a piston blew and the car sat motionless in the pits as the time ticked by and the Schuppan/Jarier Mirage closed in. 10 minutes from time Barth set out to complete two slow laps sufficient to secure victory. The car struggled across the line on its five cylinders. The win that had for so long looked out of reach, and then was nearly, so cruelly snatched from their grasp, was safe at last.

1978: Martini Porsche 936 - SECOND
Again it was Porsche versus the Alpine Renaults, but this year it was the French equipe who would be victorious. Ickx was again teamed with Pescarolo and again the top Porsche entry hit problems - gearbox. Just as before, the team leader was transferred to the other team car, driven by Wollek and Barth, which was holding fourth place behind the three Alpines. Gradually the German car clawed its way into second place but was then delayed for half and hour by gearbox malfunctions. They were therefore unable to capitalise when the leader stopped, leaving the way clear for another Alpine, the Pironi/Jaussaud example, to assume the mantle. Despite a great effort the Porsche finished five laps down. The miracle of '77 had not been repeated.

1979: Essex Porsche 936 - DNF
Paired again with Brian Redman, they were amongst the leading group when a tyre blew at around the three hours mark. Much time was lost as the Lancastrian had to limp around virtually a whole lap to the pits. The resultant damage to bodywork and cooling system took well over an hour to fix. The stage was set for another Ickx charge and he duly obliged. Within an hour of getting back to the track, they were up to 13th and by 2.15am they were seventh. Then calamity struck as an ignition belt broke, but he managed to get going again. Two hours later the stewards announced the disqualification of car 12 for outside help during its earlier difficulty and a healthy car was pushed away into retirement. It is said that a mechanic just happened to drop a replacement belt at the spot the Porsche had been stranded and Ickx had just happened to find said article

in the darkness....1979 was the year all the favourites faded away so leaving victory to a Group 5 machine. The 935 Turbo of Klaus Ludwig and the Whittington brothers was always well placed to capitalise on the bad luck of others for a well deserved win. Another 935 came second in the hands of Rolf Stommelen, Dick Barbour and the man who got all the publicity that year, movie star Paul Newman.

1980: Martini Porsche 908 - SECOND
Ickx had announced his retirement at the end of 1979 but was enticed back and teamed with Reinhold Joest. Michele Leclere practiced the car but did not take part in the race. The Ickx/Joest pairing led as they approached six hours gone but lost 15 minutes out on the circuit when a fuel injection belt came off - this time they carried spares! It took the Belgian five hours to make up the lee-way and regain the lead. There it stayed until two thirds run when Joest struggled pitwards. It was gearbox problems - the same fifth gear malfunction that had dogged the team last year. The Rondeau of its maker and Jean-Pierre Jaussaud now led, maintaining it despite a precarious off-track excursion during one of the sudden, frequent showers. Ickx drove his heart out in the final 90 minutes and managed to get the deficit below one lap. More rain: Ickx pitted for 'wets' in a last desparate gambol whilst Jaussaud stayed out on 'slicks'. It was all now in the lap of the Gods, and for once they did not smile upon Monsieur Ickx. The sky cleared, the track dried and the race was lost. The Rondeaus were first and third, the cars being built just a few miles away. The local boy had really made good!

1981: Jules Porsche 936 - FIRST
Retirement was again interrupted by the lure of Le Mans. This year the offer was to team up with his 1975 winning partner Derek Bell in the Spyder. After the usual early place-swapping sagas, they simply drove away from the field to an untroubled victory by fully 14 laps. Rondeaus were second and third - unable to repeat the glories of a year earlier. Ickx's fifth win - a new record. The event claimed the life of Lafosse plus a marshall in separate incidents.

1982: Rothmans Porsche 956 - FIRST
The introduction of Group C saw Ickx back full time. Porsche efficiency proved too much for the likes of Ford, Nimrod and Lancia while the factory team was too good for the privateers. The works cars came home first, second and third led by Ickx and Bell. As Le Mans victories go this, like last year, was an easy one.

14

is with the Rothmans Porsche that Jacky Ickx is most associated in his success of later years.

1983: Rothmans Porsche 956 - SECOND

Ickx lost a lap to the field almost immediately when pitting for new bodywork after a clash with Jan Lammers (Canon 956) at Mulsanne Corner second time around. By dusk, however, the Ickx/Bell charge had taken them into third place behind the other two Rothmans machines. The Mass/Bellof car then experienced engine problems that would lead to its eventual retirement. The team leaders closed inexorably on car 3 of Schuppan, Heywood and Holbert, only to be delayed further, by 10 minutes, with a broken electrical connection out on the circuit. After a pit stop they then dropped to six laps behind the leaders. Again they clawed their way back and with just 20 minutes to go, Derek Bell put them onto the same lap as Al Holbert. Too much distance, too little time. Starting the last lap clouds of steam billowed from the rear of the leader and Bell got ever closer. He was just 65 seconds behind at the finish - and promptly ran out of fuel. One more lap for either of them and the third placed Kremer 956 of Elliot/Andrettis could have won!

1984: Rothmans Porsche 956 - D.N.E.

The works team boycotted the race as a protest against FISA's disregard for its own reliability rules. Many observers felt the event would be downgraded but it led to one of the most unpredictable races for many years. There were nine race leaders in the first 16 hours until the Pescarolo/Ludwig Joest 956 pulled clear of the pack. The NewMan liveried car had been delayed by fuel pressure problems in the first hour and remorselessly clawed its way to the front to win by two laps. It was a fine win in true Ickx-like tradition! Second came the 'Swapshop' 956 and third the JFR example. The dreadful accident to John Sheldon (Nimrod) claimed the life of a marshall.

1985 Rothmans Porsche 962 - 10th

Joest proved they could win with or without a works challenge. This time the yellow car saw off the challenge of Palmer and Weaver (Canon GTI 956) to lead by sunset and from then on simply drove to victory, never missing a beat. The Canon car came second ahead of Bell and Stuck in the top Rothmans machine. The car shared by Ickx and Jochen Mass had a variety of early problems thereby losing over an hour of track time. Thereafter it had a troubled run to the finish - Mass also collecting fastest race lap - so was never able to mount a famous Ickx charge. The opposition was too strong and too fast. Jacky Ickx's last Le Mans finished with his worst ever finish - tenth. It was the end of an era.

The fatal accidents to Stefan Bellof and Thierry Sabine were, probably, the final acts needed to make Ickx renounce his seat in the Rothmans Porsche team and, effectively, bow out of active traditional motor sport. After all, the 41 year old had seen it all and done most of it: European Formula 2 Champion of 1967, runner-up in the F1 series for both '69 and '70, winner of eight Grand Prix races. This enviable record in single seaters is overshadowed by his stature as a sportscar driver. In 20 years the former tank instructor (!) scored some 34 major wins in the category, culminating in being crowned World Endurance Champion for both 1982 and 1983. These feats, in turn, are eclipsed by that fabulous record at just one venue: Le Mans. Jacky Ickx - ably supported by his partners, especially Derek Bell* - had set a record of achievement at the Sarthe circuit that may never be bettered. It is not just the wins, however, but the manner they, and most other attempts, were achieved. More than Foyt at 'Indy', Brock at Bathurst or Graham Hill at Monaco, Jacky Ickx's name is irrevocably linked with one place, one challenge. The closest comparison probably lies outside motor sport with Lester Piggott and The Derby. In so many ways their personalities - neither would probably be favourite to win a Mr Nice Guy competition - their professional stature and public acclaim, are parallelled. Both with their recent retirements left a void which may never be filled. Ickx's absence from the starting grid for the '86 race took away a little of the magic and anticipation from the World's greatest motor race. The King of Le Mans had abdicated but could anyone, ever, claim his crown? (KW)

*See Kimberley's Racing Driver Profile on Derek Bell.

PURPLE PHASE

When a new, big time, big buck sponsor is announced, motor racing enthusiasts tend to welcome its arrival much like a missionary dealing with a heathen: another convert to the faith. They venture out from their temples - usually some swish hotel where the official commandments have been communicated not in stone but in press literature handouts - with the well hyped message that once reduced to its most basic form translates in any language to see me, buy mine. The team and its members are garbed in their coats of many colours while the colour co-ordinated hangers-on enjoy that pagan festival of the commercial world, the corporate freebie.

After a while, said sponsor departs as quickly as he came thus leaving the space open to another marketing exercise, another evangelist extolling the virtues of his products and services. The cynical observer - and surely most ardent race fans have some modicum of that trait or they would not stand in many puddles for hours on end watching cars go round and round going nowhere - are left to ponder, should they be so disposed, as to what the sponsor actually got out of it all except some fun and a much lighter wallet or, even, why they ever got into it in the first place!

To find one company's answers to these and many other questions, I went to see the money man at motor racing's newest high profile sponsor: Mike Whitehead of Silk Cut. As the world knows by now, a factory blessed team of racing Jaguars are back in top level motor sport for the first time since the halcyon days of the fifties and since the beginning of the 1986 season, the colours of the Tom Walkinshaw run team are those of this major cigarette brand. Silk Cut, for the record, are a part of Gallaher International who, in turn, are owned by the U.S. giant American Brands conglomerate. Race fans will remember John Fitzpatrick's 956 in American 100's livery scoring a creditable fourth place at Le Mans in 1985 piloted by David Hobbs, Jo Gartner and Guy Edwards.

Gallaher International's wide range of tobacco products include such famous titles as Old Holborn, Hamlet, Condor, Senior Service and Sobranie. The other activities incorporate such diversities as Dolland & Aitchison the opticians, Rexel office equipment and Prestige household products.

The Jaguar deal is handled by Gallaher International who are the overseas marketing operation for Silk Cut products and Mike is its Marketing Manager with one hat while being the sponsorship liaison supremo with another. Our meeting, neatly timed midway between the Silverstone and Le Mans races, clearly showed that it was more than just a part of his job, Mike obviously relishing his role and the opportunity to be part of motor racing history in the making.

It was with the return of Jaguar to racing that Silk Cut became involved with motor racing. (KW)

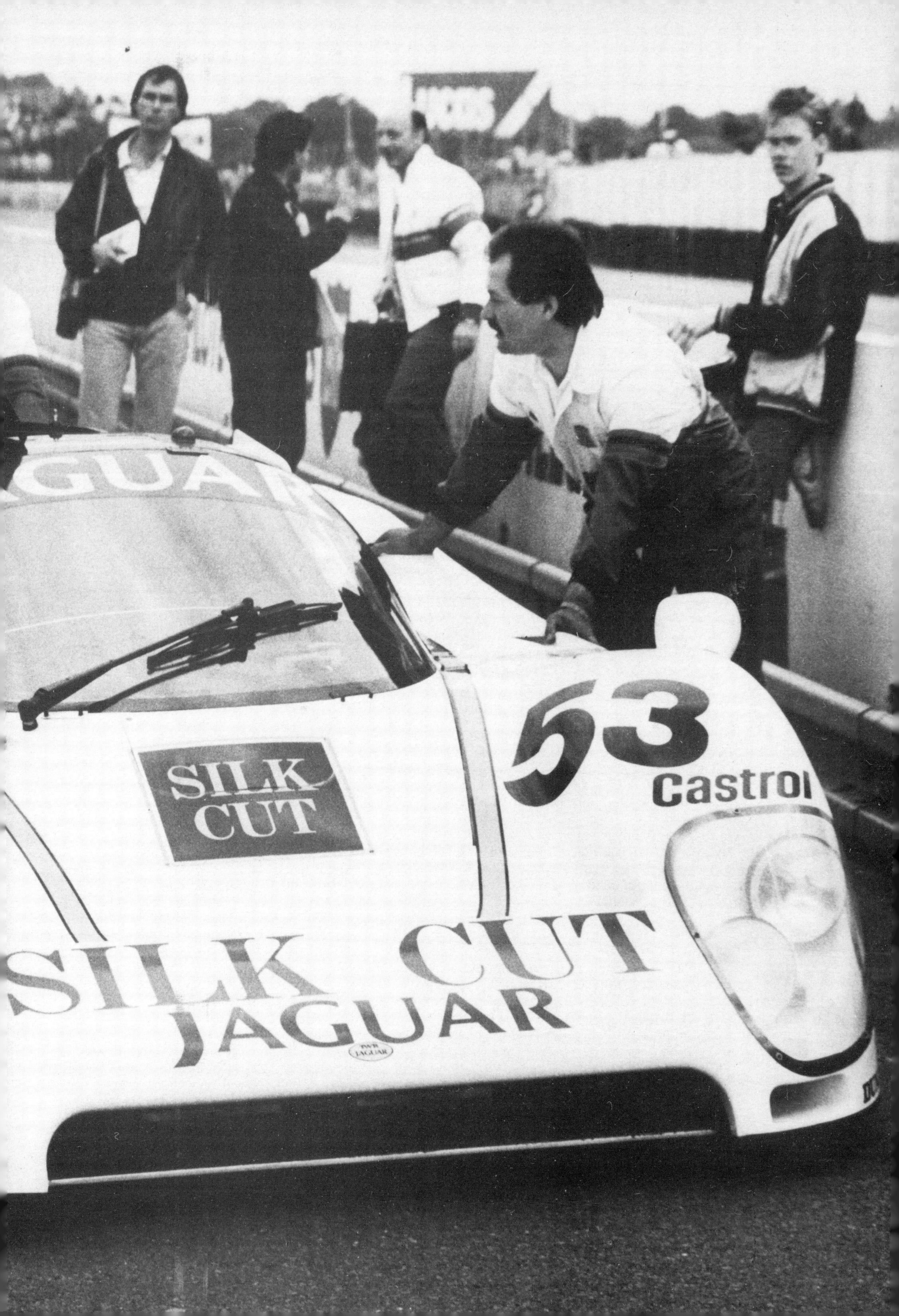
JAGUAR
SILK CUT
53
Castrol
SILK CUT
JAGUAR

As they say, the best place to start is at the beginning, so I commenced by asking why and how the initial contact came about. How did it all get started?

"We had begun to think about ways of marketing Silk Cut rather more dynamically in international markets. In broad terms we were aware of the need to invest into Silk Cut a property which was not apparently inherent in the product itself..." he commenced in pure marketing man jargonese "...and we needed to add something to that property to capture people's imagination and to stimulate consumers' awareness."

So they started to look around for opportunities to link their cigarettes to something with the right image and ingredients. Meanwhile Guy Edwards (remember him) had been charged by Jaguar to find suitable sponsors for their fledgling endurance racing team. Motor racing's legendary Mister Sponsorship knew of Silk Cut's plans and so hey presto! he became what Mike refers to as a 'marriage broker'. Since the deal was struck, Guy Edwards Racing acts as an intermediary between the parties and is also retained by Silk Cut to help them in a number of basic logistical and public relations areas.

"Most people, on thinking about our position, would probably come to the same conclusion. It represented a superb opportunity to do what we were setting out to do!" Things moved quickly despite the problems of re-arranging internal budgeting. "We put our company budgets together in July. In September we had to find a significant amount of additional money so much of our planning was disrupted to a degree in order to fund this particular project, which we were delighted to do. We re-did all the numbers and some of the things we planned to do went out of the window this year." The contract was signed and the official launch took place at London's Royal Garden Hotel in January.

The contract between Jaguar and Gallaher International is for an initial three years and does, like all similar arrangements, contain a number of mutual severance clauses. However the company is optimistic that they will be able to take up the option on a further three years. He obviously appreciates the time needed for the team to develop and to build a fully integrated promotional package around their exploits. The Jaguar name was tremendously significant.

"I think that the attraction for us of Jaguar was total. There is no other British manufacturer, speaking personally, that I can see us seriously becoming involved with in the same way that we have gone together with Jaguar."

In essence, one gets the feeling that Silk Cut cannot believe how very fortunate they were to strike up such an exciting and harmonious association with such an acclaimed, respected and prestigious name. Interestingly, there is space to let for secondary sponsorship which must represent a marvellous opportunity for someone.

Most someones tend to want to put their money into Grand Prix racing with its higher level of general interest and, most importantly, extensive television coverage. Were Silk Cut tempted to follow that path? Mike recalled a conversation with Ken Tyrrell who had telephoned earlier on in 1986 to make similar enquiries on a Formula One versus Group C basis. Mr Tyrrell, you may recall, was reported in one of the motor sport weeklies a while ago as referring to endurance as 'club racing'.

"I had to say to him that we couldn't afford it in the foreseeable future! So, in a sense, F1 was a non-starter for us although we never went into it in great depth because we wanted to become involved in a form of motor racing where we had a reasonable chance of winning something over a given three year period. The fact that Marlboro dominated that area would have been a tremendous challenge had we had the money...but we had to cut our cloth...."

At the other end of the scale they don't discount the possibility of nurturing some promising newcomer to eventual stardom.

How then does a company like this evaluate the success or otherwise of their sponsorship programme? After all, at the end of the day all they want to do is to make Joe Public choose Silk Cut in preference to another brand. What is the magic formula that decided their strategy? Is it by counting column inches in newspapers and the like? Maybe it is the simple matter of additional sales in specific markets? Or could it be that intangible of experience, good old gut feeling? The answer is very unscientific: all three! Try feeding that into your computer! The marketing man explains:

"If part of my objective was to assess, on a cost effective basis the money we are spending on Jaguar, I'm quite certain I'd go insane after about six months." He admits that they look at the media coverage obtained from a specific event as compared to their major competitors. "You don't need to be a genius to work out that we are interested in getting greater exposure than Rothmans," but has yet to action any public awareness studies regarding his cigarettes and their car.

Motor racing, like a number of sports acts as a promotional outlet to tobacco companies denied other avenues by legislation or practice. How then did the Jaguar people react to the possibilities of being thus associated?

"I wasn't a party to board meetings, but I'm quite sure, in fact I know, that there were reservations amongst senior people in Jaguar. They weren't overly strident and they didn't carry a tremendous amount of weight...There were one or two reservations expressed at shareholders meetings and other public gatherings like that - nothing that has been overwhelmingly anything for us to worry about."

It appears that the strength and commercial realism of Jaguar's chairman John Egan, and his marketing chief, Neil Johnson, were enough to overcome the anti-smoking factions and the relationship between the parties has blossomed into a firm bond in an amazingly short space of time.

The problems of being a tobacco company do not end with the signing of the contract - in many ways it is only the start. At the time of our talk the number of races proposed for this season had dwindled from about a dozen to just eight. These included two in Britain with its voluntary code of practice restricting such advertising and another pair in Germany with its forbidding legislation.

"But we knew that from the outset and have to tailor our marketing activities accordingly." Nevertheless, the more countries that impose such restrictions, the less likely the tobacco companies are to stick around. The BBC has already clashed with Rothmans over their blue lozenge on McRae's rally Metro and other identifying shapes like McLaren's red and white chevron could cause similar problems in the future. So too could the Silk Cut purple square. The fact of running in unbranded livery - sans wording - is one of the reasons there were no Silk Cut advertisements in the national press on the day after Silverstone as "to spend more money to put across an unbranded livery might be very hard and the least cost effective way of trying to achieve what we were doing."

Other factors against the celebratory adverts were the fact that the hastily revised budgets did not really allow scope for such measures and that the deal is through Gallaher's overseas division who are more interested in Bahrain than Bournemouth, Brisbane than Bridlington. Anyway, there was nothing to stop their friends in Coventry laying out for a few pages of self congratulations....

Silk Cut may be somewhat limited in

Despite all this apparent razzamatazz, the Silk Cut promotional arrangements for Le Mans are decidedly low key for it transpires that a rival French concern has a financial interest in the circuit - hence all the Gitanes paraphernalia - so restricting the obvious presence of the likes of Silk Cut in terms of banners, flags etc. Mike remains undaunted and is undoubtedly assured in his own mind that the very presence of the fabulous Jaguars, bedecked in their now familiar Silk Cut markings, will be very much the centre of everyone's attention - with or without the bunting. "It should be very exciting!"

Something else that should be exciting - even more so - is the prospect of a ride in a XJR-6. "We said: 'Look Tom, we want a day out with a few of our best customers, some time in the season, to take them around Silverstone or Brands or somewhere to scare the pants off them.' At that time we'll get the board of directors along as well. That's a jolly we've planned for ourselves taking into account the timetable the team has." Thinks: how can I become a best customer or a member of the board? Anyone out there got a light.....

As for the future beyond hurtling through Woodcote or down Paddock Hill alongside the likes of Messrs Warwick or Cheever, I asked Mike about Silk Cut's vision of the Group C future as we approach a new decade. "I want to see Rothmans stay in, I want to see Mercedes come back with a full team, a works team, as soon as possible. These are ideals of mine. My interests are what we are all trying to do. I want to see the Japanese come in because I think they will add a tremendous dimension to the sport. When that begins to happen, then the Far East programme will pick up, as a result we will get more fixtures. And I think the American side will become much more interesting. We can count ourselves extremely fortunate at being able to work with Jaguar: we hope it is the beginning of a new era in endurance racing with all the benefits we've touched on for sponsor participating companies, teams and production companies," - not forgetting the fans! - "and ultimately this could, perhaps, begin to rival Formula One in the sort of world-wide interest that has. That's a long term objective but one well worth keeping in mind." Silk Cut recognises that there is much to be done in stimulating general interest in sportscar racing when compared to the slick Grand Prix promo machine, and certainly appear willing to do their bit. What's good for them is good for Jaguar is good for Group C. (KW)

eir opportunities to push this year's xploits due to their internal financial ructuring, but will probably have a much ore outward approach next year. Their lans include the building of some replica rs that would appear in shopping centres nd the like to generate interest for their roducts and the sport, initially throughout urope but then, hopefully, on a world-ide basis. There was a car present at the pening of Heathrow's fourth terminal but e competitive demands on Tom Valkinshaw's team often precludes such rrangements - hence the need for replicas. like relates the story that Silk Cut wanted car for a few hours in Paris at their nportant press conference on the Monday rior to Le Mans. TWR said no! There are any sponsors who would not have taken o for an answer so both TWR and Jaguar an surely count themselves fortunate to ave found as understanding a partner. bviously he who pays the piper does not lways call the tune!

Some sponsors seem to want to run the hole show themselves while the recent enna/John Player/Lotus dramas show ther influences taking a dominant role. he subject of the Norfolk powerplay, erek Warwick, was subsequently signed drive the XJR-6 thus giving Silk Cut the arvellous drawcard of a British superstar a British supercar. What more could ey ask for! The fact is that they do not em to ask for too much.

"We are happy to leave the team and all at area to Tom and Jaguar, whose rerogative it is. I say happy because ey're the experts and to date they have ot together a pretty interesting team - oth the regular team and, indeed, the rivers they have managed to enlist for Le lans. We could, informally, say what out so-and-so, but in the end I'm very appy to leave that aspect to them. I think, the end of the day, that whole area, for etter or worse, is down to Tom and the aguar people," adding by way of a

footnote, "it is important for channels of communication between a sponsor and a company to be very simplistic and very plain for everybody. This is your area, this is our area. Otherwise there's hell to pay!"

The competitive showing at Monza followed by the success at Silverstone was the best possible way to consumate Guy Edwards' marriage of like minds. It had been agreed from the outset with the Jaguar people that there would be no guarantee on results during the initial year. The overall plan being "to look good, to perform well, for the drivers to be happy and for the thing to build during the course of the season. Silverstone was an amazing victory to me and one that we thoroughly deserved. We were ecstatic about it....it made me hope that we weren't getting too much too soon!"

Two rounds gone and two good performances to show for it, but the next round is the big one. Everything pales into virtual insignificance compared to Le Mans. Here is a relatively new team with their new sponsor ready and willing to take on the might of the Porsche panzer divisions in what has become their own domain. They may be ready and willing, but are they able? Anticipation of such success allied to the magic of the Sarthe race meant there was not any shortage of people offering to carry Mike Whitehead's bags.

"There are quite a few people interested in coming with us," he muses in what must rank as one of the classic understatements of the year. "We've got a whole series of suites over the pits and will be taking about a hundred people there. The numbers are getting bigger all the time!" Added to which is their own marquee in the 'Parc Reception' plus Jaguar's own entertainment facilities. "We will be mingling with them and their guests and vice-versa. So generally speaking, it should be quite a homely atmosphere." He has obviously never been to my home!

PURPLE PLAQUE

Just around the corner to the Army Museum in Chelsea sits one of motor racing's biggest guns - and like such hardware, his actions go largely unseen, but the results are explosive! Ken Wells investigates.

Guy Edwards, son of a wartime bomber pilot-cum-dentist (a drill sergeant may have been more appropriate!) has gained the enviable reputation as the sport's Mister Sponsorship with battle honours that includes such diverse combatants as Barclays Bank International, Guinness, Encyclopeadia Brittanica, I.C.I., *Penthouse* and Gillette. His latest successful campaign has been to bring Silk Cut and Jaguar together for a combined assault on the Sports-Prototype World Championship.

The invitation to visit him to talk about this arrangement in particular and his ideas apropos sponsorship in general was too good to turn down. Visitors are now rarely welcomed to this private hideaway, the very house into which he first moved when he came to London about 20 years ago. Then he was a tenant, but is now the freeholder, but lives elsewhere.

As with competitive people everywhere, the more prestigious the names and the bigger the deal, the more exciting the challenge - and the bigger the rewards. So when Jaguar first approached him in March, 1985, out of the blue, to find a commercial partner for their forthcoming Group C programme, he felt elated for even in his illustrious career, this had the potential to be the biggest yet. The man who claims that he would relish the opportunity to sell Great Britain Limited was quite sure he would succeed in the quest, the biggest question being how long it would all take. He was armed *only* with a letter of authority from John Egan (Chairman and Chief Executive) and a long treatise from Neil Johnson (then Sales and Marketing Director) into the Jaguar philosophy of the venture. Guy stresses the importance of the discourse for without the right approach to the crusade there would inevitably be conflicts of interest between the parties of any agreement. Before he could start Edwards had to know that Jaguar had the right approach to the venture and their intended partner. He had to find a company with similar attitudes and ambitions.

The first stop was at the Jaguar headquarters in Coventry where a month was spent ascertaining just who Jaguar are!

Everyman and his dog knows that the Big Cat makes cars but if someone was to be assured that the best way to invest his marketing millions was by putting it onto the bodywork of an untried and untested racing car, they would need a lot more information than that. The outcome of these labours was a slide presentation of about half-an-hour's duration featuring details of items such as Jaguar's current range, main markets, commercial aspirations, revenue income and annual profits. It showed how Jaguar is one of the most prestigious corporate names in the

world, it showed how other companies use the Jaguar machinery as a backdrop to promote their own products, be it rainwear or toiletries. It also showed some motor racing! The next step was to draw up a listing of companies and organisations that could inter-relate well with the motor manufacturer, could be so disposed towards such a plan and had both the necessary wherewithal and back-up facilities to do so. Guy subsequently selected about 100 candidates, taping great lists onto the office wall, being gleaned from the pages of appropriate writings, an

awareness of those indulging in corporate advertising on a grand scale and from his own vast experiences. This was when the action started.

Top of the list was the name of Gallahers and it was to them, or more precisely to Gallaher International, that he made his first approach. Why them? Well the whole thing can be put down to experience, common sense, good groundwork and good contacts and can, in effect, be traced back to an unsuccessful Grand Prix team with a rival cigarette manufacturer. In 1982, Guy Edwards was Commercial Director of the RAM March equipe and as such was introduced to Rothmans director Peter Gilpin by Jochen Mass. An agreement was reached that Rothmans would sponsor the team with Jochen as a driver, but neither were to last beyond one season after the disappointments of a totally undistinguished liaison. Rothmans subsequently chose to concentrate their efforts in the fledgling Group C and the rallying environment where, in the very same year, they won the Drivers' Championships in both disciplines, the W.E.C. Makes title, the [...]

Mans race, the Monte Carlo Rally....

Gilpin moved on to become Chairman
of Gallaher International. Their next joint
arrangement was for the 1985 Le Mans 24
Hours when American Brands Inc.,
Gallaher's parent company, sought a
promotional outlet in Europe and thereby
put their colours onto John Fitzpatrick's -
or whom he had previously secured the
Skoal Bandit support - Porsche 956, which
Guy helped bring home in fourth place.
Funding for the project, however, was
from this side of the pond. As an aside it is
interesting to note that the car, which bore

London's real East Enders than the
psychology degree gained at Durham
University.

With these two participations behind
them, Gilpin was an ideal candidate to
approach about Jaguar. Mister
Sponsorship knew of Mister Chairman's
plans to uprate Gallaher International's
marketing profile and as the two men had
got to know each other quite well, the first
informal approaches were made over
Sunday lunch at Edwards' home. Gilpin
was immediately interested in the prospect
but it was not just a matter of convincing

despatched some three thousand letters
touting for sponsorship but got nothing.
Guy, on the other hand, makes a personal
initial approach by telephone to ensure he
reaches the right person, usually the
Marketing Director, and can spend all day
working out *precisely* what he will say
when he makes the call...

It took until August for Gallaher
International to agree to the proposals and
Jaguar to accept Silk Cut against whom
there had been a small amount of
dissension regarding tobacco products, but
this was not allowed to influence a
commercial decision. Contracts were
signed on 7th September. He had cracked
it, first time! In fact it was the culmination
of nearly six months activity in which he
had put aside all his other projects and
devoted himself full time, often 15 hours a
day, to the Silk Cut - Jaguar cause. It had
taken about £100,000 to finalise and there
had been no guarantees that any of it
would pay off until pen was put to paper.
For the very first person ever to envisage a
Jaguar with purple markings, it must have
been a moment of supreme satisfaction.

That, however, was not the end of the
matter for Guy Edwards Racing is retained
as a promotional consultant to the team
and through his Paris office, with its dozen
or so staff, handles such items as press
releases etc. It took until the middle of
January before the official announcement
was made, the interim four months being
spent to sort out details of the promotion,
from logos to logistics.

the legend American 100's, was originally
to be designated Carlton 100's after their
U.S. based product. Rothmans, owners of
the trade name in Europe, objected, so the
very was changed. Touchy stuff
sponsorship! It was his last race before
retirement and concedes, at this juncture,
that driving gave more physical pleasure
while sponsorship hunting is more mentally
stimulating. He also reckons that his
success at the latter owes more to his
experiences selling china to the Americans
so, not *that* China despite his remarks
about G.B. Ltd!) and central heating to

the boss but, as in any large concern, the
other directors, the executives and perhaps
even the shareholders, ultimately, of the
advantages of such actions.

It should be noted that the Guy
Edwards approach is to sponsors
individually and to go through the motions
before, if rejected, moving onto the next
possibility: hence the lists. Obviously there
is a substantial risk of rejection after a
considerable amount of time and money
being expended, but that is his way - and
results speak for themselves. He recalls
that Jaguar's American operation

The writings on the wall are still there
and are now used to chase a secondary
sponsor, but as Guy acknowledges, this
can often prove harder than getting the
main contributor as nobody likes to be
second rated. It contains many names that
are crossed through, no joy, while others
are encircled as if on a shortlist.

Apparently the house will soon undergo
major refurbishment and be turned into
luxury apartments. It will mean an end to
that amazing inner sanctum, a tall and cool
room with its myriad of trophies atop filing
cabinets, its seemingly random scatterings
of motor sport paraphernalia and the cord
carpet awash with dozens and dozens of
blue manilla folders each bearing the name
of a company, a project, a dream. Outside
in the street, two nearby houses bear the
familiar blue plaques that denote the
previous occupancy of notables from the
world of the arts. Maybe, one day,
commerce will be so rewarded and motor
racing's Mister Sponsorship will warrant
such an accolade, but perhaps purple
would be more appropriate.

THE SEASON SO FAR

The fifth season of Group C racing heralded its third world title. For 1986 it would be known as the 'F.I.A. Sports-Prototype World Championship'. More significant was the inclusion of some sprint rounds amongst the traditional long distance events. Ken Wells reviews the season up to Le Mans.

In contrast to such changes, the lists of entrants and drivers looked superficially, at least, much as before. Ongoing partnerships included Rothmans for Bell and Stuck, Carma for the inseparable pairing of Finotto and Facetti, Spice for 'Gordy' and Bellm, Joest's underrated Ludwig and Barilla. ADA had director Harrower at the wheel of their Gebhardt and Brun Motorsport retained Thierry Boutsen as the only GP driver planning a full season in sports cars.

Notwithstanding, there were a number of new liaisons and ventures to be found. Most prominent was the gaudy livery of the Silk Cut Jaguars combined with the star pairing of Eddie Cheever and Derek Warwick. This was one team that did not need to seek out exposure! The Kouros-bedecked Sauber-Mercedes looked positively dour alongside. Bob Wollek replaced the retiring Jacky Ickx in the Rothmans seat. Lancia had a new pairing. Out went NewMan. In came Mickey Mouse! Amongst the C2s for the first time were the Argo-Zakspeed and Gordon Spice's glorious Fiero.

The new season started with the new format. Cancellation of Mugello's intended 1000Kms meant the season began at Monza with the inaugural sprint race. The Rothmans team were reluctant, late entrants having intended to concentrate a limited season around the longer events. Mugello changed all that! It was Ludwig's 956, however, that led from the front row and dominated the race until sidelined by clutch failure on lap 50. Bell and Stuck inherited the lead which they kept despite the spirited charge of Nannini's Lancia. An inaccurate fuel read-out had delayed the car during de Cesaris' spell sufficient to put car Numero Uno out of reach. Both cars spluttered across the finish-line out of fuel but two laps clear of the rest who were led by the three Brun Porsches. Jaguar had nothing to show for a highly competitive weekend when Warwick parked his XJR-6 with a broken driveshaft and 'Branca' suffered fuel feed problems one lap from home. Both had been in third place at the time of their respective demise. Next time, they vowed, next time....

The works Gebhardt was a very worthy winner of the C2 class. Its main rival, the Spice/Bellm Fiero, being delayed by fuel feed problems when poised to challenge for the lead. They, at least, managed to make the finish unlike the ADA Gebhardt who were closing in for a possible class win when it expired shortly before the end. Again it was the inevitable fuel feed problems. The whole race had become a mockery as its leading protagonists strove to make the finish. The sprint had become a crawl.

Silverstone, two weeks later, was a different matter. It was the venue for the first endurance race of '86 - and the only one prior to Le Mans.

The Fitzpatrick Racing, Danone sponsored Porsche 956 (above) was off the pace at Monza but showed a good fifth at Silverstone (DC). Gordon Spice's glorious Fiero (below) was the car to beat in C2. (KW)

New boys in school included the much revised Cougar, the Royale Mitsubishi, a pair of IMSA Mazdas and a V6 Metro turbo engine for the evocatively named Ecurie Ecosse. This added yet another name to the impressive list of engine suppliers in the lesser category - a class whose variety of contestants and quality of its racing often overshadows the 'big boys'.

The Unipart Lamborghini failed to appear - again. A late entry from Lancia signified their new found optimism. In total contrast, the Martini sponsored team had originally planned only to compete in a couple of the sprint events, but here they now were with 1000Kms ahead of them. Were they hoping to 'do a Rothmans' by winning a race they had not intended to run? They certainly gave it their all. For a full three hours the pole position car traded the lead with the Anglo-US driven Jaguar while the second TWR machine initially held a strong third place. When the Lancia was delayed by fuel pump problems, car 51 had an unchallenged run to the flag. Oh, what joy! Silverstone resounded to patriotic revelry not heard since 'Wattie' won the Grand Prix five years earlier.

What about the Porsches? They were left in the wake of the Lancia and the Jaguars, but despite various maladies, it was the World Champions' 962 that proved too strong for the remainder. The works Porsches were still the team to beat as Stuck struggled home, the 'trick' transmission in disarray.

Gartner, Weaver and Barilla all shone amongst the minor places and the Sauber finished again. Two out of two. Engine failure after 159 laps crippled the Ecosse when two laps clear of the Fiero. So ended the dreams of a fairy tale debut for the Metro unit. The Spice car, which had been significantly delayed early on with ignition problems, held the class lead from then to the flag for a resounding class win - five laps ahead of their 1985 chassis now campaigned by Kelmar Racing. ADA had some compensation for the Monza heartbreak with a fine third place.

IMSA/GT honours fell to the Mazda of Katayama and Terada - two laps ahead of the Fiero. All in all, a good race with a fine result. Jaguars had won their first important sports car race since the '57 Le Mans and thoughts soon turned to a possible repeat performance. The tour companies and ferry operators rubbed their hands with glee....

Before Le Mans proper, however, was the small matter of the Le Mans Test Day. And small it certainly was as most teams either missed it completely or just sent a single vehicle. TWR arrived with a full compliment of three cars - at least one

Nigel Stroud's new cars for 1986 were the Mazda 757's. (WK)

team meant business. The three were each fitted with different aerodynamic features to counter the specific demands of the Mulsanne. They were rewarded for their endeavours with first, second and fourth places on the lap times and a one-two through the speed trap. Third on the lap sheets was the Rothmans 962 for Wollek while Weaver's GTI-run Nissan proved disappointingly slow. Others present included some local Rondeaus, the older

Ecosse DFL and the new Porsche 961. Th four-wheel-drive car showed potential o this, its public debut.

The supposed sprint races proved to b non-events with only a handful o contenders, most of whom just treate them as extensions of the test sessions. Th record shows that the Rothmans Porsch won both times, first for Mass and the with Wollek aboard. Would they find it s easy three weeks hence?

Scene Setters

MONZA:
Alan Collins, the well known Essex enthusiast, was keen to know how his beloved Jaguars had fared at Monza. On the Monday morning after the event, he was dismayed to note that the 'dailies' had ignored the race so decided to phone TWR's for the full story. Their staff said they didn't know as none of the team members had yet returned to the Kidlington base. Undeterred, Alan telephoned *Autosport* to be advised by a young lady that although she was unaware of the full details, the event had been 'won by Bell and Steed!' In a Hillman Avenger...?

SILVERSTONE
Patrick Head of Williams was seen during practice in the Rothmans pit accompanied by a Japanese gentleman. Honda are

already developing an 'Indy' engine a the CART series is, after all, that for wh the 956/962 unit was originally conceiv With Mazda, Nissan and Toyota alrea into Group C, will Honda take on th fellow countrymen at Le Mans bef much longer?

SILVERSTONE
Just as the Cheever/Warwick XJ blasted away from a mid-race pitst someone further up the pitlane carrying two cups of tea to person manning the pit wall. There was a mom of sheer terror on his face as the Jag gobbled up the distance between the Arching backwards with a outstretched, the car missed him by inc - probably being doused in 'rosy lee' a went....

THE JAGUAR CHALLENGE

Qualifying for the 1986 Le Mans race provided almost as much interest as the race itself. Ken Wells explains.

Oh, how they jeered Derek Bell at Le Mans this year! The unofficial patron of the British informal society of Sarthe worshippers, was booed and heckled by his, otherwise, regular supporters - and he loved it!

It has become customary, in the pre-race festivities, for each crew to be introduced to the crowd in reverse grid order then paraded up and down the pits straight perched on the back of a cabriolet. Nearing the climax of the exercise, the loudest cheers had been for the Jaguar drivers - notably Car 51 in fifth spot - and especially vocal were those who had taken up positions opposite the T.W.R. pits. The occupants of the second row passed in relative silence to be followed by the men in the blue and white machines that headed the field.

To the British it was a surreal situation for the man they always supported, their Derek, was the living embodiment of what they regarded as the biggest threat to a dream win by Jaguar, the Rothmans Porsche team. It was, if anything, a Catch 22 situation, for they wanted Jaguar to win, but not for 'Dinger' to loose.....

Approaching the multifarious banners of the 'Big Cat' fan club, Derek stood up, proudly pointing to the logos emblazoned across the chest of his race suit. To a man, woman and child they rose to the bait: the more they shouted the more he encouraged them, the more he goaded them, the more they denounced him. Co-drivers Holbert and Stuck watched in amused amazement as their team mate orchestrated the crowd in a cameo of spirited banter, a marvellous piece of theatre.

Derek had summoned up his own position earlier in the week: "I hope the Jaguars do very well. I think they will gain a lot of experience this year, but there is no way I want a Jag to win, obviously......It'll be fairly even and, if anything, we'll have the upper hand but things go wrong in twenty four hours so who can say?".

The Porsches had the advantage in qualifying, alright, with pole position beyond the reach of the normally aspirated V12s et al who could muster no better than the third row. Everyone is adamant - particularly those who fail in its pursuit - that pole position is unimportant for such a marathon, but how they all cherish the opportunity to claim it!

The serious money was on either of the two leading works 962s, both equiped with conventional - non PDK - transmission, or the awesome 956/chassis 117 from the Joest stable. The aura and reverence that now surrounds this double Le Mans winner is almost tangible and nobody was likely to bet against it completing the hat-trick.

Serious money was on the Joest 956, chassis 117, winner of the previous two Le Mans races. (KW)

The German teams with their German cars chose three German hares (sic) for the job in hand: Hans-Joachim Stuck, Jochen Mass and Klaus Ludwig, while their co-pilots had the less enthralling tasks to perform ready for the big day.

After Wednesday's early session the World Champion held sway over the Taka-Q driver with Mass a fraction back, but after the intermission Jochen, the lap record holder, was out immediately to record a 3m15.99 his compatriots were unable to better. Hanschen's typically spectacular attempts to claim his second consecutive pole position were thwarted by a spinning C2 car and the rain showers that blighted both qualifying days. Jochen had something of a reputation for not liking Le Mans, but his front row partner was revelling in the situation, even dismissing an enquiry about his car's progress with a jocular and flippant: "No progress - no pole position!"

Meanwhile the famous yellow and white machine lurked on the second row, as it had done for the past two years....and Ludwig had the turbo-boosting, morale-boosting satisfaction of being fastest through the Mulsanne speed trap at 374kph.

Two other teams, Kremer and Nissan, had declared their intentions of trying to secure pole position, but both were destined to abandon such ideas before ever mounting any such challenge. The Kremer brothers' black Kenwood sponsored 962 was fitted with a special qualifying three litre unit, but it expired terminally after only a couple of laps, so they had to revert to a conventional 2.65 flat six to secure a disappointing 15th slot, but were expected to be more of a threat in the race than their practice dramas had suggested. Sadly, it was not to be.

Kremer's - and just about everybody else's - practice woes pailed into insignificance when compared to the Nissan debacle, neither of whose cars outqualified the aged Porsche 936 of Schuster, Seher and Siggi Brun - for whom the latter complained that they had experienced a misfire, damper problems and a chassis that was totally out of balance - but still they managed to outpace the Nissans! Nor would the Japanese have even claimed the C2 pole position for their best effort left them a full second adrift of the remarkable Spice Fiero.

The hierarchy had decided to bring one of the new R86V machines and an '85 model such as had won at Fuji last October, with James Weaver, who had done the testing of both machines, curiously allocated to the older car. Then, even more curiously, came the decision from Tokyo that he was not to drive at all - it would be an all Nippon effort.

The Japanese drivers, with their extremely limited experience of the Sarthe between them, then proceeded to go their own way despite the combined efforts and formidable talents of Keith Greene (contracted from Richard Lloyd's GTI concern), James Gresham and Gordon Coppuck. The car that was recording 203mph under Silverstone's *Daily Express* bridge could manage no more than 185 at the end of the Mulsanne.

The Japanese elements of the team seemed totally overawed by the fearsome reputation of Le Mans but were often going totally against the decisions of the man regarded by many as the best team manager in the game.

The adage that 'East is East and West is West, and never the twain shall meet' never seemed more appropriate, but in the earthy atmosphere of the paddock one team member put it more succinctly: "If we went for a swim in Slough Sewage Works we'd be in less s..t. Things are not good - and slowly geeting worse. How on earth the Americans got duffed up at Pearl Harbor is beyond me!" You could tell he was not a happy man!

Things, however, did improve on Thursday - after some heated exchanges for which formal translation was superfluous - and Weaver was reinstated to the driving force, promptly setting a time a full six seconds quicker than the other occupants of car no. 32, but all it was good for was the 17th row alongside Richard Cleare's IMSA March 85G, ironically an almost identical chassis, but a much less favourable power-to-weight ratio. The R86V could only manage 25th spot - a long way from pole - with a best time less than six seconds ahead of the Englishman. In pre-race testing in England, James had taken the new car around a full seven seconds quicker than the old, so on that basis the R86V should have been some ten per cent up on its older sister - equivalent to a start from the fourth row at worst.

It is easy to conclude that the Nissan saga was a result of translation problems and/or cultural differences, but it was a truly soul-destroying episode for such respected professionals as they were virtually powerless to stop their Oriental masters commit competitive hari-kiri. A definite case of Mulsanne Madness!

It is reasonable to assume that one day Nissan will be at the right end of the grid, but they will not do so without reflecting deeply on this weekend of lost opportunity, and when they do, hopefully they will acknowledge the debt owed to March, Keith Greene and the others for endeavouring to set them on the right path.

Jaguar had no such aspirations of pole position - the lack of turbocharger putting paid to any such flights of fancy - and their problems were much more mundane. They started with loose undertrays on all three cars that had to be hurriedly reinforced before getting down to the serious business at hand. There was an air of guarded optimism in the camp, but deep inside they knew it was a little like trying to climb Mount Everest blindfolded: each step forward being a step in the dark, into the unknown. Their successes at other venues during the last year counted for nowt, TWR's experience at the Spa 24 Hours saloon car race being an entirely different matter. This was different, this was Le Mans. It would be a long uphill struggle if they were to enjoy the rarified atmosphere of victory and echo Sir Edmund Hilary's immortal line: "We knocked the bugger off!"

Eddie Cheever appreciated the difficulty of the task, commenting on Thursday lunchtime: "We qualified fourth, but I don't think we will remain in that position. If we start in the first six I'd be happy. Today we are working on the race with the race engine in, now we have to try and pick up in four hours what Porsche have done in 20 years so it will be very difficult."

Win Percy, meanwhile, was his normal ebullient self and happy to be a part of it all: "I've wanted to drive one for some time, but the normal reaction from Tom is 'No, stick to saloons'. He's relented at last."

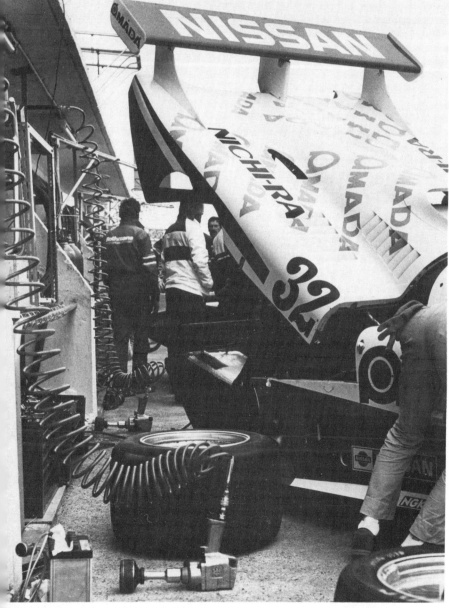

The Kenwood sponsored Porsche 962 (opposite top) was fitted with a special qualifying three ...re unit for practice, but that expired after only two laps. (KW). Everyone turned their back on ...e Nissan R86V (opposite bottom) after their disappointing practice. (KW). The Nissan R85V ...bove) qualified even lower. (KW). 1986 European Touring Champion Wm Percy (right) ...ove one of the Silk Cut Jaguars. (KW)

Ivan Capelli would probably have shared Winston's enthusiasm if sponsorship clashes had not precluded such a deal thereby allowing Armin Hahne to join the squad in a car he had never driven before at a circuit he had never competed at before! Their car suffered brake problems which delayed its programme and progress so consigning it to start amongst the pack from row seven.

Someone who had driven the car before and had no such worries about the novelty of the track was Derek Warwick when he reminisced about his 1983 exploits with the CK5: "It was a really s..t car and no resemblance to this car at all. The only thing it helped is I know which way the circuit goes!"

The new Brabham Formula One pilot had to give best to his American partner on Wednesday while on the second day, Cheever was 'rested' when Warwick and Schlesser - an evocative name in French motorsport - undertook the race set-up tests. These they accomplished admirably, ably backed up by car no. 52 notably through the efforts of Hans Heyer.

The threat to Porsche looked more than just a fanciful whim. The cars were fast and stable, their consumption rate well within a competitive target, so it all started to fuel the speculation that if, just, maybe..

This was the team that everyone had come to see and many hoped would end Porsche's domination at the Sarthe. They had done it at Silverstone, so why not at Le Mans? The difficulty of the task, however, was indeed much more complex than that. It was not just a simple matter of a multiplication factor of the variables involved, but more akin to the Richter Scale used by seismologists to assess earthquakes whereby Scale Five is not a fraction more severe than Scale Four, but double it, Scale Six being double Scale Five and so on. The magnitude of Tom Walkinshaw Racing's efforts could be similarly calculated for where the Silverstone win took less than five hours, Le Mans was a full 24...or as Eddie Cheever had indicated, it was four hours versus 20 years. The hope remained however - could Jaguar turn the Silverstone tremble into an earth-shattering experience for the Porsches at Le Mans?

Although Rothmans and Silk Cut seemed to be hogging most of the attention, it was Kouros whose Sauber chassised/Mercedes engined challenge stared down at everybody from the

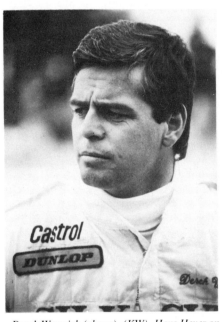

Derek Warwick (above). (KW). Hans Heyer on the limit in practice (above right). (DC). Danner set the quickest qualifying time for the Sauber team in car no. 62 (below right). (DC)

dvertising hoardings and out from the rogramme's cover. Since arriving on the roup C scene earlier in the year, they had ven their name to both previous rounds f the championship: at Monza and ilverstone, and were now involved in the romotion of their home event.

For Le Mans there were, for the first me, two of the C8 models with saloon car ce Dieter Quester and 1985 Formula 3000 hampion Christian Danner seconded to e trio that came eighth at Silverstone. anner showed obvious pleasure at being e team's fastest qualifier but priorities ere not on practice positions, but on aintaining their 100% finishing record nd with quadruple winner Henri escarolo amongst its formidable line-up, ey represented a veiled threat to the ore fancied runners if the dark blue achines were still around at the end.

The only other non-Porsches in the top 20 were the Primagaz Cougar with its 956 engine and the Secateva WM powered by its Peugeot V6. The car from Stuttgart-en-France was, in fact, built by the local Porsche dealer Yves Courage, being sponsored, like the second Kremer Porsche, by Primagaz and recorded an excellent 10th on the grid through the inspired efforts of Alain de Cadenet and Raphanel, the French Formula 3 Champion having a tail damaging spin in the wet of Wednesday's qualifying. The WM was four rows further back despite being second only to Ludwig through the speed trap set up at Hunaudieres - this giving further credence to the accusations that the car, which only appears at Le Mans, is a 'Mulsanne Special'.

Brun Motorsport are gradually becoming a more potent force to be

reckoned with in Group C, with the ample talents of Thierry Boutsen and the underrated Larrauri to lead their challenge. While most used the second day for race testing, the Swiss team chose Thursday to clock their best times with the Arrows F1 star recording the day's best at 3m20.10 with the Argentinian some three seconds back in second place on the time sheets. This was enough to give them fourth and sixth respectively on the grid with the team's patron back in 12th place adjacent to car no. 8. Of all the other 956/962 derivatives, the most noticeable was the second Joest entry in its Stars 'n' Strips livery of Old Glory. Despite not having the pace of its famous sister, only 11th on the grid, a trouble-free run could reckon to bring new glories to the trio fronted by former Can-Am Champion, George Follmer.

The Primagaz Cougar (above) was one of only 7 non Porsches to qualify in the top 20 and found itself on excellent 10th on the grid. (DC). The second Kremer car (left) qualified 22nd. (DC)

The Richard Lloyd 956GTI had a terrible first day of practice (below) but finally claimed a respectable 16th spot. (DC). Immediately behind the Liqui-Moly car on the grid was the John Fitzpatrick Porsche of Alliott/Romero/Trolle/Konrad (right). (KW)

Richard Lloyd was less than pleased after the first day of practice and described the 28th position of the 956GTI machine as: "Bloody awful. We had a myriad of problems, basically handling, and we have also got two drivers who haven't been here before, which doesn't help. Today we have made a lot of changes and I am pretty sure that we will get it right. There is a bit of a problem with the Goodyear tyres as well but I think that they know what the problem is so we live in hope." With his faith in Mauro Baldi and the charity of a clear run, the GTI boss was finally rewarded with a much more respectable 16th spot after sterling work by the diminutive Italian.

Immediately behind the Liqui-Moly sponsored car came the first of the John Fitzpatrick Racing (JFR) Porsches led by Phillipe Alliot, but it was Franz Konrad, seconded to the team only on Thursday afternoon, who posted their grid time - but did not participate in the race. Meanwhile there were substitutions afoot in Fitzpatrick's Danone car too when veteran Juan Fernandez stood down in favour of young Fouche. Mickey Mouse lined up in 19th place!

The remaining C1 cars mixe[d] themselves amongst the C2 machines qui[te] liberally. The two Toyotas suffered fro[m] only having 500 horsepower to play wi[th] while a pair of Rondeaus were evocativ[e] reminders of their constructor so tragica[lly] killed in a railway crossing accident just s[ix] months before. The final qualifier in th[e] top category was Costas Los' Meta[xa] March: despite the efforts of Dermagne [to] destroy it and then proceeding to driv[e] back to the pits, split oil radiator and all, [to] report on his adventures. The Frenchma[n] was given his marching orders and replace[d]

The Dome Toyota (above) suffered from only having 500 horsepower to play with (KW) while Costas Los' Metaxa March (right) was the final qualifier in the top category. (KW)

by the dependable Neil Crang when his Tiga Turbo drive went the way of its new engine and Tim Lee-Davey's team did not qualify.

At Silverstone, both the Mazdaspeed 757s, with their triple rotor motors, had finished while Richard Cleare's March had claimed fastest race lap before its early demise. So the stage was set for a fine battle in the IMSA GTP category between the Japanese machines designed by Nigel Stroud, who was also responsible for the special 956GTI chassis, and the 'previously owned' car of the archetypal British amateur enthusiast.

As per their previous encounter, the Mazdas outqualified the 85G which also suffered the pain of having its nose rubbed in the dirt at the end of the Mulsanne. Fractionally slower than the best Mazda was the sole contender for the IMSA GTX

class: the dramatic new Porsche 961. First seen at the Test Day earlier in the month, it represented the first four-wheeled drive car to contest the event - and how the project team prayed that the heavens would rain down everything short of plague and pestilence so as to enable it to challenge its more prototype cousins at the front of the field. The fact that the 961 people wanted rain and hail, snow and storm was somewhat ironic for the vehicle was the tarmac derivative of the Paris-Dakar 959 where the conditions were more of hot, arid deserts. Driving the 961 were triple 'Raid' winner Rene Metge, who had shown his track prowess by wins such as the 1983 Tourist Trophy, and Claude Ballot-Lena who was participating in his 21st consecutive Le Mans. If anyone could get the new machine to the finish it was this pair. There was disappointment in some

quarters that it had not been even quicke but 3m43.45 was no disgrace so early int the project and only about 15 second down on the Ickx/Bell pole time of 1982. I the powers that be allow it to develop, could create a storm in the future, while the REAL powers that be created a storm during the race, it could get its jus rewards.

The only other non-C car was th Belgian BMW M1 and qualified by forme F2 man Pascal Witmeur.

The M1 shared the back row with th Ecosse DFL that had been the C pacesetter 12 months ago. It, like its ne Rover-engined stablemate, was driven i *sotto voce* mode with the sole intention c still being around come the finish, with th Ray Mallock/Richard Williams led tea having a brand new V6 flown in priva aeroplane on Friday - there's class for you to be installed for the start.

In the GTP class, the Richard Cleare March 85G (below) was outqualified by the two Mazda's (top right). (DC). The Porsche 961 (centre right) was the first four-wheeled car to compete at Le Mans and qualified 27th. (DC). The Ecosse DFL (bottom right), the C2 pacesetter of 1985, qualified on the back row. (KW)

This year's C2 pacesetters were Spice Engineering and their fabulous Fiero which was less than a second away from embarrassing the Primagaz 956 while suitably humbling the efforts of Nissan, Mazda and Toyota from the, supposedly, quicker categories. The loss of a door on Wednesday was nothing but an inconvenience while clutch problems were a portent of dramas to come.

Second in the C2 class was the pink Cossiaud Rondeau, albeit two rows and three seconds adrift of Spice & Co., which had the additional satisfaction of out-qualifying its two big sisters thanks to

Bruno Sotty's inspiration on Wednesday.

Alongside the C2 Rondeau was the works Gebhardt with its mentor much in evidence while the older example campaigned by English privateers from Ian Harrower's ADA concern were not at all concerned to be seven rows behind their own personal yardstick. Anyway, the ADA example with its patriotic paintwork complete with a Union Jack on the central fin looked prettier.

Less pretty was the C2 Secateva WM, so classed because it ran with a less powerful, and subsequently more economical, Peugeot V6 but, for sure, this

year team patron Roger Dorchy would not have the satisfaction of leading the race for a couple of glorious laps as he had in 1984.

Next in class came the first of the BMW-engined contestants, the vivid Bassaler Sauber which just pipped Jens Winther's Castrol URD for whom David Mercer out-ran his employer by a mere half second.

The other Bavarian engine was to be found in the little ALD of Paris PR man Louis Descartes who must have hoped that for once he would have some good publicity to announce come Sunday afternoon.

The works Gebhardt (above left) qualified third in class while the older example (top right) found itself several rows behind. (KW). The BMW-engined ALD qualified in 46th place alongside The Tiga-Ford GC 86 (above right). (DC). The top BMW-engined qualifier was the Bassaler Sauber (right). (KW)

The BMW M1 (far let) was the last qualifier. (DC)

The heart of the matter (right). (DC)

The vivid stars 'n' stripes of car no. 8. (DC)

The Hall/Andrews/Bain Tiga-Ford was destined to last only five minutes in the race, parked on lap 2 with drive shaft failure. (DC). What can one say? (left)

Roy Baker joined the exclusive band of entrants with three cars. The Tiga-Ford GC84 of Thomas/Musetti/Allison (left) qualified 48th and the Nicholson/Sheldon/Thyrring GC86 (above) qualified 45th. (KW). More Cosworth hardware provided the impetus for the Alba (below), the only Italian car to be entered this year. (DC)

Ford were making plenty of copy from the fact that it was 20 years since the thunderous Mark 2s first won at the Sarthe, but these days their presence is less Detroit Iron and more Northampton Nikasil.

Roy Baker joined the exclusive band of entrants with three cars and they were all powered by 1700cc BDT engines. Nevertheless, qualifying had been relatively painless so after the calamities of the season's earlier two races, all they could wish for was that the three car set-up at the third race would mean third time lucky.

More Cosworth hardware provided the impetus for the Alba, the only Italian car to be entered this year, and the Bardon nee Arundel that replaced John Bartlett's fated Chevron. With 12 engines on the starting grid that could be traced back to his pen, the legend of Keith Duckworth's brilliance continues to shine. The great man's name could in no way be tarnished by the fact that the head gasket went on the Italians' red DFL while the Goodmans Speakers sponsored car looked good - and so did their bikini-clad lovelies.

There would be silence in the Strandell pit on race day as, for the second year in succession, they failed to make the grade - and to make matters worse, they were over 3 seconds down on 1985! Beset by a multitude of problems they never, ever looked like beating the count. Observing a team member daubing on its number '106' in the pit lane, armed with a pot of red paint, one wondered as to the preparation standards of the troublesome machine.

Rallycross ace Martin Schanche had left the Strandell organisation at the end of last season to set up his own C2 team utilising a Zakspeed turbo engine allied to an Argo chassis similar to that which had done so well in the USA. He was full of praise for the abilities of David Kennedy who had set the car up following its rebuild as a result of the Silverstone indiscretion.

"He was very professional. Everytime he came in he said do this, next time do that. Everytime he went out the times sunk. All the time, so..... He's one of the tops. If you stuff him into a 962, he can show his calibre. At the moment he is not a winner."

As for his own chances in the race the Norwegian's optimism was apparent on Thursday with the response: "I think there will be a quite a few blue faces before the finish, so let's wait and see!" By Saturday morning, though, it was he who was looking blue as he reported that their only engine had been damaged by a cracked water pipe and the outlook was anything but rosy.

The Strandell (top failed to qualify for the second year in succession. If the standard of painting on the door (above; was anything to go by, it was of little surprise. (KW). Rallycross ace Martin Schanche (on the left in the picture on the right) entered and ran his own Argo-Zakspeed.

Overleaf: The sister cars of Joest Racing represented the greatest threat to both the works Porsche and Jaguars. (DC)

So the 50 cars took their places for the 54th *Vingt Quatre Heures du Mans*. There would be many a private battle fought out in the most public of arenas. There would be success and failure, sadness and joy, for they are the very ingredients, the very essence, of this annual festival of sport and drama. Throughout the circuit, throughout France, throughout the world, people had their own favourites and their own vested interests. There were thousands of questions that would all be answered come this time tomorrow. One question was paramount, though: could Jaguar win Le Mans?

8

JOEST
RACING

GOODYEAR

JOEST

G. FOLLMER
J. MORTON
K. MILLER

JOEST RACING

BP

BP

BP

SACHS

8

PORSCHE

GOODYEAR

BOSCH

THE FRENCH RESISTANCE

While it is the winners who receive all the glory, there are still 50 or more other entrants who are making as much effort as they can despite the fact that some know they stand little chance of a class win let alone outright victory. Some teams put in as much effort just to qualify only to fall at the first fence. Ken Wells stayed near the Tim Lee-Davey Tiga team pit during their heartbreaking attempt to defeat not just the time barrier, but also the French organisation.

One of the most disheartening sights at this year's Le Mans was that of watching the mechanics working to change the engine on Tim Lee-Davey's Tiga C1 car while knowing that their efforts would probably be in vain. The job completed in the early hours of Saturday morning, the crew managed to snatch a few well earned hours of rest before pushing the Unipart Supreme/Penthouse liveried machine the length of the paddock to the pitlane gates. Their hope was that they would be permitted to take up their position, while the arguments, about whether or not they would be allowed to start, wrangled on. The officials adopted a 'they shall not pass' attitude so after some exchanges of Franglais, the team had no choice but to push the car back again. It would spend the race as an adornment to the Unipart promotional office in the paddock - an ignominious end to a week that started with such optimism.

The chassis taken to Le Mans was Tim's regular GC84 as the newer one had not been completed in time. Tim commented: "The chassis, last year, we felt was marginally better than the Porsche, which frankly isn't that hard - the Porsche chassis isn't its strong point. The chassis is not as good as the Jaguar, but it is good enough to do the job we need."

The big thing with this project, though, is not the chassis but the engine. Conceived by Graham Dale-Jones and developed by Terry Hoyle, it is a twin-turbocharged Cosworth 3.3DFL. The most noticeable feature of the unit is the fact that it has separate four cylinder distributors mounted at the end of each bank and had completed some 30 hours on the dyno with encouraging results. However the inevitable delays inherent in such an advanced project allied to some installation problems meant that the car had not been tested nor moved under its own power before arriving at Le Mans.

As Howden Ganley - himself second in the 1972 race - commented: "When it was wheeled out of the shop it was turning its wheels!" The Tiga boss was adamant that the Cosworth turbo is the right path to follow on the basis that: "If you were going to any engine designer in the world to build the best engine for a category, whatever it is, who is the man? I think it's Keith Duckworth." Indeed this is possibly the engine that Cosworth's themselves may have evolved for the Ford C100 if that project, for which it was destined, had not been aborted.

Tim Lee-Davey echoes Ganley's enthusiasm: "I believe that for sports car racing it is the best engine you could possibly have. If the engine's inherent advantage is sufficient to overcome the lack of finance compared to Rothmans Porsche or Silk Cut Jaguar, we feel the engine can do the job and we feel, therefore, the team can do the job. So let's go for it."

Tim Lee-Davey's Tiga C1 car fell foul of French officialdom and failed to qualify. (KW)

Thus spoke a bravely optimisti[c] man. With no disrespect or intention t[o] decry his efforts intended, there are man[y] who would say Tim Lee - Who? And her[e] he was boldly predicting the possibilit[y] that, during the course of the three yea[r] programme, he may well take on the migh[t] of Porsche and Jaguar and come out o[n] top: he could succeed where the likes [of] Lancia, Aston Martin-Nimrod and WM[-] Peugeot had failed. Will the star of BBC['s] 'The Big Time' be treated to a happ[y] Hollywood ending?

Wednesday's qualifying sessions wer[e] more traumatic than any script writer coul[d] ever envisage. On its very first lap, the ca[r] left the pits, got as far as the Dunlop Curv[e] and stopped. There it stayed until th[e] intermission! During the second part of th[e] day's activities Lee-Davey managed a fe[w] laps before, once again, they wer[e] sidelined by more problems. He explaine[d]: "We have got one or two little teethin[g] troubles. There is something that [is] stopping it giving the power that it gives o[n] the bed - possibly in the managemen[t] system somewhere. We had one sid[e] running leaner than the other at one poin[t] so we are fairly cautious about it all...S[o] long as we don't get any major dramas, o[n] the performance we have got already, th[e] car will qualify so don't read too much int[o]

he lap times it's done at the moment - it's only done six laps!"

Major dramas did visit Team Tiga like a spectre of mechanical doom when the engine let go in a comprehensive manner on Thursday. It had, during its brief life, proved a very impressive sight, but not so much by its track exploits but the dull red glow that emanated from it in the darkness that follows a Sarthe sunset. The official cause of the problems were subsequently put at a broken cylinder liner.

Neil Crang and John Gimbel had both had turns in the car before its demise, but as it transpired only Neil Crang of the three had qualified under the detailed and specific regulations appertaining to this unique event. The amiable Aussie could not drive the car single-handed, so it was up to Tim to try and persuade the stewards, using all his expertise as a barrister, to allow them to race under the provision of *force majeure*; the scope for such stewards' discretion being flexibly defined in the rules.

For all of Friday and into Saturday morning TL-D could be seen rushing about the paddock to achieve his aims. Meanwhile the mechanics, led by John McNeil who had literally only been able to snatch a couple of hours sleep each night for the past fortnight or so in his efforts to get the car ready for Le Mans, set about removing the turbo lump and installing a Nicholson 3.9 DFL in its place. Incidentally, it apparently takes about 17 hours to install a turbo engine! Unfortunately all their efforts were to be in vain and most of the team resigned themselves to being spectators instead, while Neil Crang himself secured a drive in a Cosmik March by way of consolation.

There were no such rewards for Lee-Davey who then had the job of explaining to sponsors as to why their perfectly healthy car was not out there. When we caught up with him on Sunday, he was still uptight about it all. "The organisers were just French really. They came up with a set of conditions; if we fulfilled those we could run the car. It meant putting a different driver in. When we did that they changed their minds. We did that four times. We had the stewards saying they wouldn't consider the question and the Chief Steward saying: 'Keep trying to find a new driver and we'll consider it.' Basically French organisation lived up to its normal reputation. The Chief Steward, Alain Bertaud, was very helpful, but what annoys me, for instance, is they said John Gimbel wasn't quick enough so he couldn't run. The driver immediately quicker than him was allowed to run (Tourol-Cosmik March) and the driver behind him was allowed to run (Vanoli-Taverna Alba), but he wasn't quick enough!

"Then we had a French driver sent to us by one of the organisers - in fairness not a steward - who hadn't raced for two years!" At this point it was feared that TL-D might go the way of his turbo and explode, the frustration and bitter disappointment still strong.

Once his anger had subsided, he succinctly explained: "We left ourselves exposed by needing to rely on the organisers' discretion. As soon as you're in that situation your'e very open to this sort of thing. It makes life unnecessarily difficult."

No doubt he would be back in 1987 to try again, a little older, a little wiser; but at that moment Tim looked more drained than the majority of those who had been competing for a day and a night. What had he got to show for the week? Nothing.

Except, that is, that a couple of days before, his wife had presented him with a baby daughter. The mention of them brought a smile to his jaded features and the heartfelt comment: "I really don't want to be here at all!"

And, who knows, when Little Miss Tiga first goes to school, she may be able to boast: "My daddy's a Le Mans winner."

Ray Mallock. (DC)

Drake Olsen. (DC)

George Follmer. (KW)

Oscar Larrauri. (DC)

David Leslie in the Ecosse-Rover. (KW)

The JFR Elkron 956. (KW)

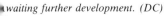

awaiting further development. (DC)

The Micky Mouse 956. (DC)

K. LUDWIG
P. BARILLA
J. WINTER

BP

JOEST

Reinhold Joest oversees his charge (left and above). (KW)

The Mazda's lined up in formation. (KW)

The Spice Fiero with Ray Bell in front who went on to break the C2 lap record. (KW)

CAR COMPARISONS

rian Redman is one of the few people who have been rivileged to drive the powerful Jaguar sports prototypes of oth Group 44 and TWR. When asked at Le Mans to ompare the two versions he replied: "It's very hard to make ny comparisons as this car is in low downforce trim for Le Mans; it has only got 50% of its normal downforce. The ngine is powerful - it appears to have rather a narrower ower band than the American engine but feels more owerful in that powerband. I guess that the weight of the car lso helps the acceleration as it is 100lbs lighter than the merican car due to the rules. The downforce actually oesn't feel so much different to the way that we (Group 44) ormally run. This car has just a bit too much downforce at e front at the moment, the tail is a bit light under braking nd on the fast kink on the straight. Otherwise it feels omfortable and quite easy to drive".

The popular Lancastrian, forever unlucky at Le Mans, is ne of the few drivers left in top line motorsport whose career ncludes the legendary Ford GT40 and the fabulous Porsche

Brian Redman.
(DC)

ackie Oliver and Thierry Boutsen. (DC)

917. One of his contemporaries is Jackie Oliver who now heads the Arrows team in Grand Prix racing and was present on Thursday in company with his F1 protege Thierry Boutsen whose Brun 962 was destined for the second row on the grid. Oliver won Le Mans in 1969 in a Gulf GT40 while his time of 3m18.4 aboard a 917K two years later still stands as the fastest ever race lap at the venue. He seemed the ideal person to recall those heady days and judge the modern machinery from his experiences.

"I can't remember, it was far too long ago!"he claimed before continuing: "Yes, I remember winning it. In the middle of the night it's better to be in bed!..... The 917K was the better car to drive..... I don't pay much attention to sports car racing - Formula One people are a little bit blinkered unfortunately".

Someone with a much healthier approach to the current Sports-Prototype scene is Oliver's former Shadow team mate George Follmer. At Le Mans he was driving the second string Joest 956 and would eventually be rewarded with third place. However he is probably more famous as a Can Am champion aboard the awesome Porsche 917 Turbo.

The veteran reflected: "The turbo had a lot more horsepower but the dynamics of this car (the 956) are a lot better and for that it's a lot faster. My top speed with those 917s was in the neighbourhood of 200mph on most of the road courses in the U.S where we ran them; here at Le Mans we're looking at over 230, so there has to be an improvement someplace!"

With such a positive attitude one could hardly claim that he was a Shadow of his Follmer self!

URD ABOUT LE MANS

The basis of this story is how one small Danish racing team, running on a budget smaller than some Thundersports teams run on, took part in, and finished second in Group C2 in the 1986 Le Mans race. Dave Cundy reports.

The Team: Jens Winther Racing.
Jens Winther Racing consists of a completely voluntary force of very keen, unpaid helpers plus the man himself, Jens Winther, who is Team Manager, Team Owner and for good measure, one of the drivers in the team. Included among this close knit team is Winther's wife. All of its members admit to loving the atmosphere of long distance endurance racing and although they did not really expect to compete at Le Mans this year, all the team wanted to go, indeed, they all begged to go.

The charisma of Jens Winther himself is such that to help him out, the Porsche team collected a spare windscreen from Stuttgart for him and delivered it to Le Mans while Peter Sauber collected four spare brake discs and delivered them to him at the race. When he attended the annual BRDC end of year shindig in 1985, Gordon Spice approached him to enquire about his plans for the '86 season and on hearing that he intended to stop racing as of the end of 1985, Spice did his best to persuade Winther to change his mind and continue racing. Fortunately he decided to continue for one more year principally so as to try once again finishing at Le Mans.

The Drivers: Jens Winther, David Mercer and Lars Viggo.
Jens Winther.
The progression of Jens Winther racing driver is interesting in that he has always set himself a target to achieve and then done his best to achieve the target in the shortest possible order. In 1962 and 1971 he was Danish Champion. He has taken part in 13 Monte Carlo rallies, winning Group 2 in 1977. Interestingly, in 1980 he was teamed up with Lars Viggo, who co-drove with him in this year's Le Mans, and they won the Tour d'Europe Rally overall. He also won the European Group B championship in 1983.

His final challenge to himself was to finish in the Le Mans 24 hour race, but he admitted before the race that it would be very difficult. If he was to finish, he would retire at the end of the season as he would then be 48 years old and he felt that it would be time to give up.

The Jens Winther URD. (DC)

URD was damaged in the Gartner accident having its headlight smashed.
Although Viggo refused to carry on the
race, he and Winther are still firm friends.

The Car: - URD-BMW

The URD-BMW was built in Stuttgart in
1982 and as such is thought by Jens
Winther to be the first Group C car to be
built, and was definitely the first Group C
car to be shown at the exhibition in Essen.
On being questioned as to whether or not a
replacement car had been sought at any
time, the reply was short and to the point.
In Winther's own words "Last year we
were fourth in the World Championship
and then David Mercer and I looked
around in England for another car, but to
buy a good car would cost forty thousand
pounds and for a small Danish racing team
it's too much money. After paying that
amount for the car another ten thousand
would be needed to pay for the installation
of the BMW engine which is another
problem as the BMW engine is so long. So
we said alright we will not win the World
Championship even if we do spend all that
money, so we may as well carry on with the
same car. Last year when nothing happened to the car during a race we always
finished third it was so good and reliable."

Although Winther receives a little help
on the engine front from BMW he reserves
most of his gratitude to Castrol for their
support.

Practice.

The BMW engine in the URD is so
powerful that although the chassis does not
have the ground effects of the more up to
date C2 cars what is lost in the corners at
Le Mans is made up to a certain extent
down the Mulsanne Straight. Often it
overtakes two or three other C2 cars
according to Winther. This was confirmed
by the timing line at Hunaudieres, the
URD being the fourth quickest C2 car
through the speed trap at 309kmh, slower
than the WM and Rondeau which both
recorded a time of 327kmh, and the Spice
Fiero which set a time of 325kmh. In
qualifying the URD was 38th overall on
the grid and 7th of the C2 cars with a time
of 3 minutes 53.85 seconds. The fastest car
was inevitably the Spice Fiero with 3
minutes 46.47 seconds.

Both Winther and Mercer were within
tenths of a second of one another in
qualifying, Winther recording a time of 3
minutes 54.37 seconds and Mercer a best of
3 minutes 53.85 seconds. The time set by
Viggo was somewhat slower at 4 minutes
5.40 seconds.

David Mercer

Since 1983 David Mercer and Jens Winther
have driven together as a team and their
styles have complimented one another,
both driving fast but with a view to
conserving the car. It was while driving the
ex-Ronnie Peterson Group 5 BMW 320
that Jens Winther first noticed Mercer's
driving. In 1982 Winther drove a BMW
M1, and on the look-out for another
co-driver, approached Mercer as the new
regulations coming into force outlawed the
Group 6 car he was racing at that time. The
partnership was formed there and then
with Winther being impressed that Mercer
had not damaged a car while racing.

Lars Viggo

Lars Viggo and Jens Winther have been
friends for a very long time competing on a
number of Monte Carlo Rallies and several
Tours d'Europe events together. It took a
long time for Winther to persuade Viggo to
compete in this year's Le Mans as two
years previously, when he was co-driving a
BMW M1 with Winther, he was behind
John Sheldon when he had his enormous
accident. This year he was following Jo
Gartner when the Kremer Porsche 962
went out of control and Gartner was killed,
whereupon Viggo pulled into the pits and
refused to carry on the race, leaving
Winther and Mercer to finish the race. The

In Winther's own words: "Practice was perfect so we are very happy. We will drive safely in the race. We have been doing about 310kmh on the straight, but will only go to a maximum of 8000rpm in the race and lift off twice on the straight as well to allow the engine to breathe a bit."

Opposite: Jens Winther. (DC)

By the end of the race, the URD was second in class and 11th overall. (DC)

The Race.

David Mercer was the first driver. Although electronic troubles occured on the first lap they finished the first hour in 37th place overall, eighth in class and settled down for a long race. After two hours of racing they had moved up to 32nd overall and fifth in C2 just behind the Rondeau and WM. Everything was going very smoothly. After 3 hours they had dropped a place to the second Ecosse car driven by Delano/Petery/Hotchkiss.

In the fourth hour they were overtaken by the troubled Spice Fiero, but in turn they re-took the second Ecosse and the Dorchy/ Pessiot/Haldi WM which was also in trouble in the pits. They were now running 29th overall and fifth in class once again. At the end of the fifth hour the Mallock/Wilds/Leslie Ecosse led the C2 class on 72 laps with the URD on lap 70 fourth in class, 27th overall. The quarter distance mark came and went with the car still fourth in C2 just ahead of the Spice Fiero. After the seventh hour, they were third in class and 24th overall, but the long grind of night Le Mans had set in.

Eight hours gone and there was no change in class position, but the car was now 22nd overall. By the end of the ninth hour it had moved to second in class behind the Ecosse which was leading the class by eight laps at that time.

The URD was leading by one lap the eventual class winning Gebhardt JC843 of Ian Harrower/Evan Clements/Tom Dodd-Noble, and in this fashion ran, like the proverbial train, through to half distance.

By the time of the Gartner accident the URD had dropped to third in class behind the Ecosse and the Gebhardt but had moved up to 17th overall completing 156 laps compared to the 159 of the class leader. The Ecosse was soon to drop back, however, when Mike Wilds lost the car on some oil at the chicane and was hit by the Jochen Mass Rothmans Porsche 962.

At three quarters distance the car was now 13th overall and second in class behind the Gebhardt which had completed 232 laps, six more than the URD. Next man up, the Dorchy/Pessiot/Haldi WM, had completed 217 laps.

The URD now settled down to 12th or 13th place for the rest of the race, but in the last hour moved up to 11th overall when the Elgh/Gabbiani/Suzuki Dome Toyota 86C had trouble.

So after 24 hours they had accomplished what they set out to do - finish the race. Not only that they had finished 11th overall and second in class, covering 309 laps at an average speed of 174.436kmh. The class winning Gebhardt covered 317 laps at an averag speed of 178.948kmh and was classified eighth.

It was Jens Winther who was the happiest man at Le Mans at the end of the race an amateur within the sport but setting truly professional standards for himself and his team.

GOOD OL' BOYS

There were no fewer than 17 US drivers at this year's Le Mans - almost double the number present 12 months ago. Ken Wells reports.

There has been much said and written recently apropos the marked drop in the number of Americans visiting Europe this year. The main reasons given for the stay-away being the decline in value of the mighty 'greenback' and the fear of being caught up in some terrorist action or other.

It was therefore gratifying to welcome the 17 American drivers whose participation did much to alleviate the disappointment that no North American teams had entered for the 1986 event. The Camaros and the like always give that extra little something to the Le Mans atmosphere and one hopes that they, or their successors, will return soon.

Also absent were the Group 44 Jaguars who had done so much to put the British marque back on the Le Mans map before deciding to concentrate on thir IMSA commitments and leave the Group C race to their Group C cousins, the Silk Cut Jaguar XJR-6s. Should the powers that be ever resolve the conflict of interests between the two parties, one relishes the prospect of a fully integrated assault once again from 'across the pond' with the likes of the fabulous Lola Corvette and the Ford Mustang Probe.

20 years ago Ford broke the European domination of the Sarthe race when Mk 2s filled the top three places. That year with the Mk 2s, the GT40s and the dramatic Chaparral 2D, there were 14 American 'big bangers' - plus a couple of Chevy V8-engined Bizzarinis to add to the thunder. Let's hope it does not take another 20 years to see a similar spectacle.

Of the 17 drivers present - the Magnificent Seventeen - the man who headed the list in terms of stature surely must be the driver of car Number One, Al Holbert. The 39-year old was a previous winner having had that dramatic steam cloud finish in 1983 to which he added a second victory to his list of achievements this year. Earlier in the season he was a member of the team that won the classic Daytona 24 Hours and is reigning IMSA GT Champion - a championship he was to win again in 1986. Al's father took part in the 1961 Le Mans race and scored a creditable fifth place along with Masten Gregory in a Porsche RS 61/4, but Holbert Senior was not, in truth, over-enamoured with his experience so young Al had to discover the magic of Le Mans not on the parental knee, but for himself.

When he is not actually racing, Al Holbert is Porsche's motorsport supremo for North America and therefore has a significant responsibility to the success of the marque on that continent. It was he who was asked by Stuttgart to provide a short list of candidates for the position of extra team driver at Le Mans.

Al Holbert, in car No 1, drove to victory in the race for the second time in his career. (DC)

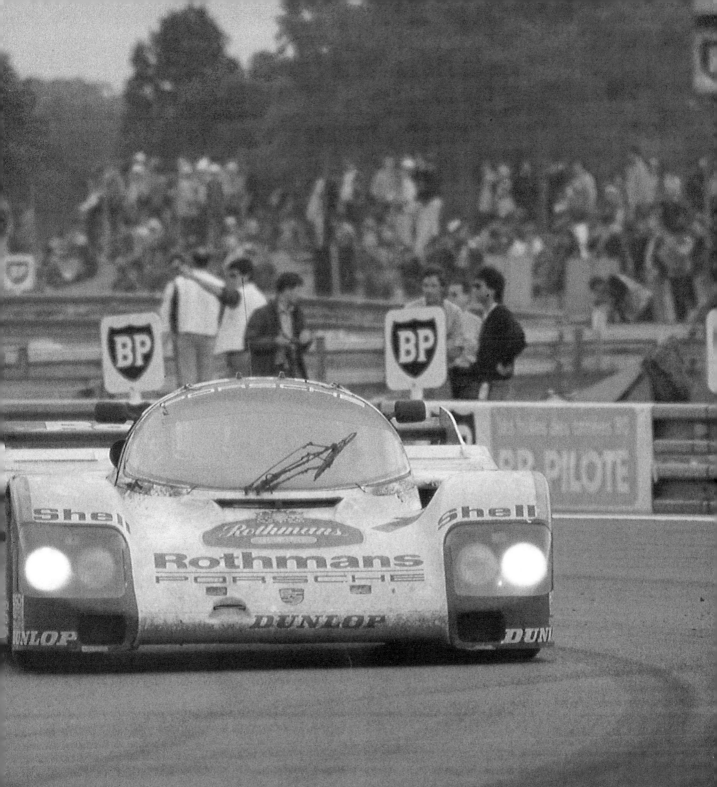

Drake Olsen's race, in car No 3, lasted only until the third hour of the race. (DC)

Out of the 'four or five' he nominated the factory chose Drake Olsen, a young coming-man in the best American tradition, whose only previous Le Mans experience was for the Nimrod team in 1984 when he was involved in the horrific accident that befell team mate John Sheldon and eliminated both cars before sunset. There was speculation that he might drive at Le Mans for Richard Lloyd, but during the Monza sprint meeting (where he came fifth with Thierry Boutsen in a Brun 962C) he was asked to partner Vern Schuppan in the PDK-transmission car. The Connecticut driver accepted Herr Falk's offer with relish, stating on race morning: "It is a very good opportunity, it's a privilege to drive for the factory, but I have a job to do and I am going to do it to the best of my ability. There's some work to get down to yet...I have a long day ahead of me!"

Unfortunately in only the third hour of the race, and after only 30 minutes of his stint, Olsen spun the car at Indianapolis when handily placed in fifth spot. Soon afterwards a gearbox input shaft snapped and Olsen's race was run. The Le Mans arrangement was a one-off deal so it will be interesting to see if the factory employ his talents again. The best person to assess h abilities is probably his co-driver an Schuppan had nothing but praise for th Rothmans rookie.

If Al Holbert was the titular head of th American dream then surely the spiritua head was veteran George Follmer in th second Joest entry. The 52-year old wa lead driver in the 'Star Spangled Banne coloured No. 8 which bore the legen 'Spirit of America'. The car wa undoubtedly one of the most eye-catchin creations present and the mello Californian enjoyed his return to the bi time.

The 'Star Spangled Banner' car No. 8 of Follmer/Morton/Miller. (DC)

It is 13 years now since, as CanAm champion, he made his Grand Prix debut in a Shadow DN1 at Kyalami - incidentally Shadow's debut too! - and was promptly rewarded with sixth place. At the next event, the Spanish GP, he gained a stubborn third place. If F1 was seemingly so easy, it all went wrong from thereon in and as the cars got less and less competitive, George failed to pick up another point all season. His F1 career ended, appropriately, at Watkins Glen where the only satisfaction to be derived was that of both qualifying and finishing ahead of his team leader, the vastly more experienced Jacky Oliver.

Since those heady days, he has settled for the less frenetic world of IROC and TransAm, Silverstone being his first venture into the big league (where he came sixth) in a modern top line racer. He had raced at Le Mans once before - "I've tried to stay away ever since" - but the Dino 206 expired, like its two sister cars, within a very short time "so I had a good night's sleep." This year, Follmer's nocturnal arrangements were not so cosy as accompanied by compatriots John Morton, himself a former TransAm champ, and Kenper Miller, they survived a couple of anxious moments to score a great third place finish for their consortium of sponsors.

Also in the 956/962 category were IMSA buddies Price Cobb and Rob Dyson who were sharing the RLR/Liqui-Moly car

with Mauro Baldi. Both newcomers to Le Mans, they were not helped by a myriad of practice problems but overcame all trials and tribulations to claim ninth spot by the finish.

Jaguar had two Americans amongst their ranks - three if you count the almost permanent resident Brian Redman! Eddie Cheever was back at the Sarthe for the first time since 1981 when he shared a Lancia Beta Montecarlo to eighth place with Carlo Facetti and Michele Alboreto. Still only 28, the no-nonsense Cheever still aspires to add to the formidable list of having driven in Grands Prix for six different teams. Diametrically opposed to Eddie in character and career was Hurley Heywood, the Chicagoan having his ninth participation dovetailed into his commitments for the Group 44 team. Twice a winner, with Porsche in 1977 and 1983, he also lists four Daytona and two Sebring 12 Hour victories amongst his achievements. None of the Jaguars made it to the finish.

Someone who did make it to the finish - and in some style - was Jack Newsum who helped Lionel Robert and team chief Richard Cleare clinch the IMSA class and 14th overall. A splendid effort.

Then there was the other all-American three man team of Les Delano, Andy Petery and John Hotchkiss who came one place further back in the older, DFV-powered Ecosse known as 'Henry'. Their combined ages, totalling over 152 years,

made them the oldest crew in the race. They struggled on after exhaust problems etc. to a worthy finish and claim fourth in class for their efforts.

All the other American runners were to be found in Tiga-chassised machines. Mike Allison and Tom Frank joined British stuntman Val Musetti in one of Roy Baker's 1700cc turbo-engined cars while Nick Nicholson was having his second Le Mans outing in a second RB Racing entry. Neither vehicle was destined to finish. At least they fared better, though, than John Gimbel in Tim Lee-Davey's Cosworth turbo-powered machine. After a succession of dramas - as reported elsewhere in this publication - the team failed to qualify and Gimbel's weekend was over before it had truly started.

Thus the story of the Americans at Le Mans this year ran the full gamut of emotion from DNQ to spraying champagne from the victory rostrum. Hopefully those who did not savour success will not become disheartened and will return next time. One of the abiding memories of the 1986 event has been the enthusiasm and pleasure of the American competitors, some of whom seemed to be able to call George Follmer a mere youngster! So maybe in 25 years or so the likes of Drake Olsen will still be battling it out at Le Mans, and perhaps the son of a 1986 points scorer will mount the rostrum to be proclaimed a winner. We'll just have to wait and see.

Eddie Cheever with Derek Warwick. (DC)

FITNESS AND FAST FOOD

Endurance racing is by the very virtue of its name a test of strength and stamina. This applies not only to the vehicles, but also to the intrepid pilots. There is a quantum leap foward in the physical and mental effort required to race competitively and safely the more excessive the duration of the event. The most daunting of all the circuit races are that exclusive little band of 24 Hour marathons such as Spa and Snetterton for saloons, Daytona and Le Mans for sportscars. Each has its own requirements and foibles, but the problems of racing at the Sarthe, highlighted by the fearsome reputation of the Mulsanne Straight, must make it the most forbidding of all.

It is, therefore, imperative that a driver gets himself fit in both body and soul for the rigours of the heat, the noise, the indomitable concentration and the lack of sleep. It is also important to be able to rest during such an arduous event. To this end a straw poll was conducted amongst some of the combatants and their response follows. Read into them what you will.

Derek Bell: "With difficulty! I was racing in America on Monday so I've a lot of jet-lag....it was very hard racing two and a half hours on my own. It was 90°F, very hot and hard, so I haven't been able to get into shape as well as I normally would. I think I'm in race shape because I won the Daytona 24 Hours two months ago and I've run since then in a race or two so I suppose I'm in reasonable condition. I just do a lot of exercise...and pretty clever about what I eat with our doctor...I don't go out boozing and that sort of thing and get smashed all the time. I have a few beers occasionally, but I'm very relaxed. We change, have a wash if possible, a massage, try to eat something and try to relax. I've never slept yet. This year I might because there are three of us in the car. It would be quite useful to sleep!"

Mike Wilds: "For the last six months I've trained three nights a week, weight training, doing a bit of running. Whether it is actually any good I don't know, but psychologically if you've done it you feel better with yourself and it tends to help your mental attitude towards the race....I have a nice restful time in the motorhome and relax. The adrenalin is going so much I can't sleep. I get a nice good cup of tea, take the wet overalls off and stick the feet up!"

Derek Warwick: "Hamburgers, hot dogs, chips, greasy buns! I don't do anything special, I just go on a diet. I eat lots of varied food to keep the stamina up. What else can you do?"

George Follmer: "Conditioning is the most important - the physical and mental conditioning. Physically I use weights, that sort of exercise. Mentally you just have to do it."

Vern Schuppan: "I keep thinking that I should start training, but I never do. I've been planning to do it for about ten years. I'll start running next year...."

Sarel van der Merwe: "No different from any other race really. The no sleep doesn't really worry me as I have got a rallying background and you spend a lot of nights awake in a rally car. So I suppose you have to try and get in as much sleep beforehand but it's one of those things you can't build up and keep in reserve. In the off sessions...you can do a lot of relaxing. I just lie down and do nothing!"

Hans-Joachim Stuck: "Get fit? I'm always fit!"

ATTITUDES AND ALARUMS

SAREL van der MERWE: "I think it is fantastic here, I love the track. You really know you are going fast- one of the very few tracks where you sit at top speed for quite a few seconds, like thirty or forty seconds. There is a long time to rest down the Mulsanne, you know, in the sense that you are not actually working. You're just sitting there with your foot flat on the accelerator as opposed to changing gears and braking. It's not a very tiring track, it's very nice".

VERN SCHUPPAN: " I wouldn't come here unless I was in one of these cars (Porsche 962) or a car that had a good chance of winning. I don't particularly like 24 hour races. I'm not saying I don't look forward to coming to Le Mans - I like coming here - but one 24 hour race a year is enough!".

THIERRY BOUTSEN: "Anyone can get a licence and take part in the Le Mans race and that is very dangerous. They should change that because you come behind drivers that have got no experience and don't know what they are doing on the track. They don't know where it goes and we sometimes come past by over 100mph - and they don't look in their mirrors! It is very, very dangerous. It's more than a mobile chicane....."

JAMES WEAVER : "With nine hundred horsepower you don't have to be the world's greatest driver to do a good lap time around here. You've got three-and-a-half miles of straight down that way, another couple of miles back up to Indianapolis, a long old drag up to the Porsche Curve and it's pretty quick past here (pointing to the pits straight). So you can almost take tea and read a book around the corners. So when you get a car that is good around the corners as well......".
and
"There is no question that when you first come to Le Mans it is a pretty intimidating experience. It's so fast and bumpy and it comes at you at a million miles an hour. It's just frightening and that is all there is to it..... The first time I came to Le Mans I terrified myself. I thought: I don't want to be a racing driver, you have got to be mental to come here. The guardrail down the straight is set in sand so if you bump into that it is a definite health hazard! It is just going to fall over and I don't want to be a lumberjack - not at 200mph anyway!".

NEW TECHNOLOGY

Excluding the likes of the Spice C2 and the Jaguar XJR-6 as variations on a theme, there were few chassis models and/or engine types that had not ventured to the Sarthe before.

One of the most interesting of the newcomers was the Rover V6 ensconced in the back of an Ecosse, the first combination of which had led its class at Silverstone only to be denied a debut win by a broken valve spring.

The V6 weighs in at about 30kgs below the ubiquitous Cosworth V8 and is said to put out 410bhp from its three litres. Development is by John Dunn's Swindon Engines from the unit that took Tony Pond's Metro to third place in the 1985 RAC Rally. The team had two brand new engines, one for practice and the other for the race.

Someone who did not have the luxury of a spare unit was Martin Schanche who used a 1800cc Zakspeed turbocharged straight four that benefited from the German manufacturer's Formula One efforts. It is mated to a Jo Marquant designed Argo chassis similar to those which cleaned up the 'Camel Lights' category in the 1985 IMSA series. The tub had been substantially repaired from its Silverstone shunt.

Another new car this year was, in fact, already secondhand! The Bardon DB/01 is the new title for the machine that Anson built a couple of years ago and named the Arundel after its mentor. Sadly the talented aristocrat retired from the sport shortly afterwards due to personal commitments and the pleasant looking C2 was put on ice until Messrs. Bartlett and Donovan purchased the project. The Goodmans-liveried car made it to Le Mans which was more than the interesting Mitsubishi-powered Royale achieved - despite statements to the contrary on BBC television, unless I'm greatly mistaken...

Someone who may have felt the trip to Le Mans was a mistake is Tim Lee-Davey who brought along his unique Terry Hoyle built DFL Turbo, but the Tiga team, as described elsewhere in this issue, suffered from their lack of pre-testing and were destined not to qualify.

The most notable newcomer for this year's race was the revolutionary Porsche 961 which thus became the first four-wheel drive vehicle to attempt the *Vingt Quatre Heures*. It is the tarmac version of the 959 Paris-Dakar 'Raid' winner and was first seen publicly in this trim at the Le Mans Test Day. The engine is a 2847cc flat six with twin turbochargers and developing up to 680bhp transmitted through a six speed gearbox via an electronically controlled clutch. It is this that varies the torque split front-and-rear amongst the four programme modes depending on the prevailing conditions. All this clever stuff can be over-ridden at the flick of a switch to get rear drive only if circumstances demand. The 961 features anti-lock brakes with ventilated discs and weighs in a hefty 1150kgs. At the Test Day it proved disappointing by not breaking 3m47.1, but this was put down to overcooling and modifications were in order for the big event. Its competitive debut was awaited with great interest - and so was the rain!

Porsche had another interesting development at Le Mans for the first time in the form of the PDK transmission. This device was fitted to the third Rothmans 962C and both drivers stressed the fact that it made the car physically less demanding than its conventional counterpart. The system allows for preselected clutchless gearchanges, the penalty for which is more weight, but although proving less reliable than the Stuttgart people are used to, was used by Bell and Stuck to win at Monza earlier this season.

It was not a memorable year for new technology, 961 apart, but the future development of all these first timers will be watched with interest. Perhaps a Zakspeed-engined Bardon fitted with 4WD and PDK was needed - now that really would have been something novel!

The most notable newcomer for this year's race was the revolutionary Porsche 961. (DC)

SARTHE SNIPPETS

It is 10 years since Gijs van Lennep scored his second Le Mans win. Added to which is his second place in '74 and the victory, shared with Helmut Marko, in 1971, that still stands as the greatest ever distance covered during the *Vingt-Quatre Heures*. Gijs also scored the first F1 points for both Ensign and Williams chassis during his eight GP appearances. History seems to dismiss the Dutchman as a lightweight, but there are plenty out there who would surely swap their results for his.....
Decals on Mike Thackwell's helmet bear allegiance to 'The Salvation Army'. Come and join us?

When was the last occasion that there was no Italian model vying for outright honours?

The badge says what, the cam cover says not! The Spice Fiero was confirming its affinity with Pontiac but running a 3.3 Cosworth DFL. A Chevy with a Ford on top?

Jaguar recruit Hans Heyer has now driven in a dozen Le Mans races without ever reaching the finish. XJ13?

They should have awarded a special prix d'endurance to the press man weighed down by no less than seven cameras.

Endurance fans seem to reckon that whi G.P.s are now saturated with casu observers, only REAL enthusiasts go Group C events. Furthermore only di hard *afficionados* attend practice session With this in mind it was interesting observe a little scene at a paddock snac bar during the break between Wednesday two sessions. Amongst those awaiting to served was a tall, lithe figure complete wi racing overalls emblazoned with multitude of decals. No deference w shown to him and upon his departure o middle-aged local turned to your intrep reporter to ask the identity of the driver. had to tell him it was Hans-Joachim. Stu for a name?

The Spanish had an excellent Le Mans, highlighted by the dogged second place of Jesus Pareja - eighth last year - in the Fortuna car of Brun Motorsport. Fourth place went to Marbella resident John Fitzpatrick's Danone-Porsche Espana 956 with Fermin Velez and former Grand Prix racer Emilio de Villota aboard. The third seat was to have been for Juan Fernandez but the veteran withdrew after a couple of practice laps as he felt too slow. Fernandez held the accolade, until this year, of being the highest placed Spanish finisher ever with his fifth place at the wheel of a 908/3 back in 1973. De Villota described the result as 'For us it's like a dream...I think this result is good for Spain and Spanish motor racing fans.' With a Group C round scheduled for Jerez two months after Le Mans the timing could hardly have been better.

uring the race, two miscreants were ptured by gendarmes shortly after ming out of a Tiga caravan. They said ey were looking for stickers!

hen Capelli's deal fell through Armin ahne was seconded to the Jaguar team to are Car No.53 with fellow E.T.C./ C.C. exponents Brancatelli and Win rcy. This prompted the Dorset lad to mark that TWR had entered two Jags d a Rover!

he DFV powered Ecosse was named enry as in Ford, while the Metro-engined ample was Reggie as in Rover!

Kouros had a massive promo campaign for the race with billboards, magazine adverts etc. On Friday, they specially chartered a train to bring down over 400 guests from Paris which doubled as an exclusive private hotel with its sleeping compartments and buffet cars. There was also a huge marquee in the 'Parc Reception' with silver service for smoked salmon, caviar etc. Unfortunately the focus of their attentions, the two Sauber-Mercedes, both spoilt the party by retiring early. Hopefully this setback will not deter Kouros from continuing their involvement in a superb and significant effort.

The hours before the start of the 24 Hours are a time of festival and ballyhoo. There are aerobatic displays and historic parades, parachutists and pretty girls. It is the latter that inevitably steal the show with the famous Hawaiian Tropic lovelies as much a reason for being there as any lil'ol' racing car. They wave and bounce and strut their stuff, they flash and flaunt and tease and taunt. For some Freudian reason it bruises the male ego to realise that the whole episode is orchestrated by a couple of American P.R. men issuing instructions like 'Okay, more waving to the left', 'Now smile to the balcony' etc., etc...

is year the public face - and much more sides - of the shampoo or sun-tan lotion mpany or whatever Hawaiian Tropic ay be were ably supported by the gals m Goodman Speakers. Will this mean her companies using the same *modus erandi* in the future? A case of where T leads...

There are two distinct categories of driver at Le Mans: those who are paid and those who pay. Although precise figures are difficult to confirm and each deal different, it appears that the average going rate for a renta-drive is about £20,000 while if you wish to have a 956 in your colours, it will set you back around £100,000.

The pitlane firemen looked very smart in their dark blue uniforms, shirt with tie and kepi. With the recent tragedy of Elio de Angelis and last year's Hockenheim refueling fires still fresh in the memory one wonders as to why these officials did not wear fireproof apparel.

The end of the race always signals the start of the orgy of looting (all pillage, no rape?) which leaves nothing sacred. Anything and everything was fair game for the souvenir hunters - except, that is, the name board over the Cougar pit which also showed its race number : 13. Are the vandals superstitious?

On Saturday morning Derek Warwick was overheard explaining to Thierry Boutsen that driving the XJR-6, as opposed to a Porsche, was like comparing a thoroughbred to a horse........

It is reliably estimated that one-third of the crowd at this year's race was British. More 'Brits' went to Le Mans than went to Silverstone!

Tiff Needell was one of those who missed out this year. The much delayed Unipart-Lamborghini project meant he was too late to find a seat elsewhere despite talks with both Kremer and Fitzpatrick. Remember those laps of glory in the Emka in 1985?

The first car home at this year's Willhire 24 Hours saloon car race - a future classic - was the Smith/Abbott Escort RST. Its 1849 miles was the equivalent of 220 laps of Le Mans - and there were seats for three passengers!

John Nielsen, the Kouros pilot, (almost literally in 1984 with his involuntary flying act) carries the legend 'There is no substitute to victory' on his overalls. Maybe next time...

When George Fouche was seconded to the Fizpatrick/Danone 956 in place of the veteran Juan Fernandez he immediately became a statistic. For the South African, at twenty one, became the youngest driver in the race. George is now in his third season of Group C having initially been with the Obermaier set-up before switching to Kremer mid-way through '8... He scored eight finishes in the points for the Köln-based brothers - including fifth Le Mans - before personality problems resulted in his split from the team. A year in the wilderness has done nothing to blunt his abilities and a fine drive, fraught with turbo and suspension problems, was rewarded with an excellent fourth place.

The orange and blue bands on Derek Bell's crash helmet recalls earlier days with an earlier Porsche. They are the colours of Gulf Oil made famous by J.W Automotive for whom 'Dinger' drove the Sarthe in 1971. The 917LH, shared with the great Jo Siffert, led early on before falling back into eventual retirement on Sunday morning. After a variety of colour schemes earlier in his career, Derek settled for the Gulf pattern and retains it to this day. A marvellous link with the great days of Seppi and Pedro, Masta Kink and the REAL Maison Blanche

The best sponsored car at Le Mans must have been the Spice Fiero. Its livery bore allegiance to Holts, Cannon Rubber, Listerine, Avon, Jaeger, Mobil, Groundspeed, Stylistick, Redex, Hawaiian Tropic and, of course, GM Pontiac. Second at Monza and first at Silverstone, the reigning C2 champions were favourites to repeat their class winning success of last year. From the C2 'pole' they were already one-and-a-half minutes ahead after only an hour's racing. Then a succession of clutch problems delayed them severely, but at least they were still running at the end to pick up valuable championship points. There was also the satisfaction of a superb new lap record - a full 10 seconds under David Leslie's time last year for Ecosse. The Silverstone-based equipe remains the team to beat in the category: the best recipe for keeping sponsors happy!

The striking pink Blanchet Locate Rondeau was having at least its seventh Le Mans race! It was, apparently, the same chassis that came third in 1980 when the sister car of Rondeau and Jaussaud scored such a memorable victory for the Frenchman. The winning car took part in an emotive tribute to Jean Rondau prior to this year's event.

The influx of Japanese media people was huge and reflected their increased level of participation this year. The very first Japanese effort was a Mazda rotary-engined Chevron B16 for Deprez and Vernaeve back in 1971. It lasted just three hours before the engine broke.

Jacques Goudchaux must surely rank as the least experienced driver in the race. The 22 year old former karter only started in Formula Ford last year coming second in the French championship. This season he continues in the Graff Racing team and for Le Mans shared Jean-Phillipe Grand's Rondeau DFL with his mentor and TV man Marc Menant to 13th place despite the additional problems caused by operating the 'In Car' television camera for Channel 5. A harmless spin made the coverage even more exciting!

During the post race mayhem four 'Brits' staged a ten yards sprint race on the pit straight. No doubt the victor will now proudly boast of the time he won a race at Le Mans........

Its amazing to watch the dexterity with which Hans Heyer removes his crash helmet and puts on his famous pork-pie hat all in one movement. Is he hiding something from us?

The British were the only ones actually to sing along to their National Anthem when it was played prior to the race start.

A soft drink spotted in a Boulogne supermarket costing under fifteen francs for a pack of eight was on sale at the circuit for ten francs each! you know what to do next time!

THE FRENCH CHALLENGERS – a pictorial look

The Cougar C12 (top) of Courage/de Cadenet/Raphanel qualified 10th, finished 18th. The Secateva WM (above) of Raulet/Pignard/Miqault – qualified 18th, D.N.F. (DC). The Primagaz Porsche 956 (left) of Yver/Striebig/Olivar qualified 22nd, D.N.F. (KW)

The Rossiaud Rondeau M379 (opposite top) of del Bello/Sotty/Rossiaud qualified 28th, finished 17th. The Graff Racing Rondeau M482 (opposite centre) of Grand/Grandchaux/Menant qualified 32nd, finished 13th. The Secateva WM P85 (opposite bottom) of Dorchy/Pessiot/Haldi qualified 35th, finished 12th. (DC). The Rondeau M382 (above) of Oudet/Justice qualified 37th, D.N.F. (KW). The Bassaler Sauber C6 (left) of Bassaler/Lacaud/Tapy qualified 38th, not classified. (DC). The Descartes ALD O2 (below) of Descartes/Heuclin qualified 46th, D.N.F. (DC)

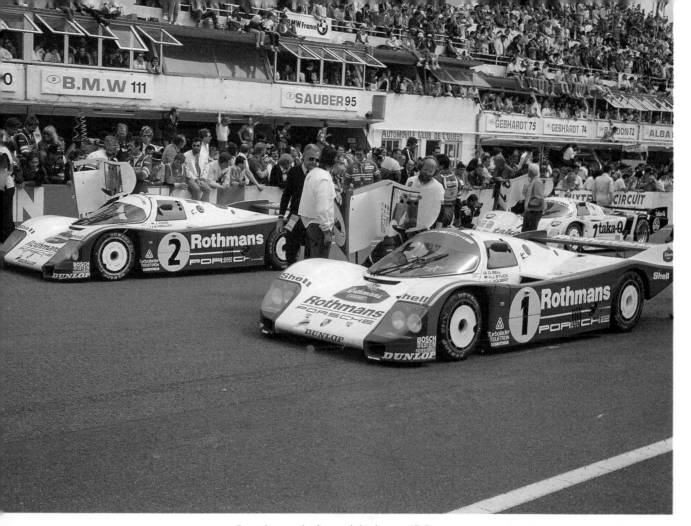

Countdown – the first and third rows. (DC)

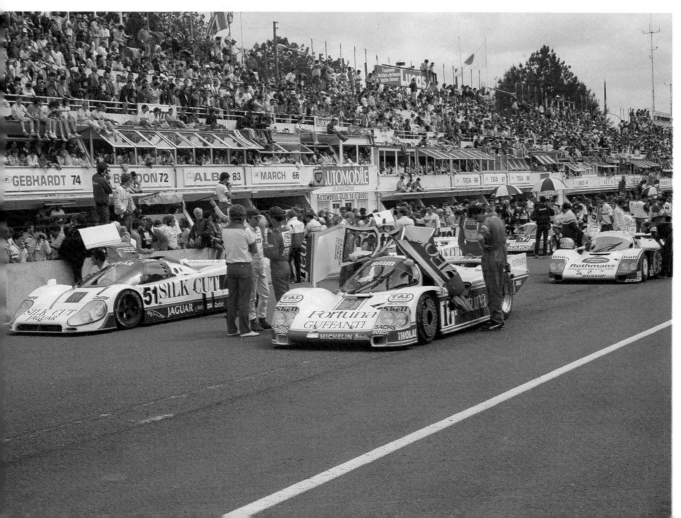

After practice and before the race. The Rothmans Porsche car No. 1 started from the front row. (DC)

Lower down the grid, the Frank/Musetti/Allison Tiga-Ford GC84 is lined up before the start. (DC)

The BMW M1 trundles its way up the pit lane to join the last row of the grid. (DC)

The Mickey Mouse 956 (opposite top) and works Gebhardt (opposite bottom) before the start. (KW)

Overleaf: The Start! Ludwig, driving Car No. 7, screamed past the works Porsches when the flag dropped and by the time they reached the first corner, it was Ludwig from Wollek and Stuck. The lead war maintained all the way round the first lap. (DC)

THE RACE

Initially the cars were lined up angled to the concrete pit lane wall, evoking memories of the famous Le Mans starts of yore. The two hours before the off are traditionally a time of festival and fun, parachutists and parades.

For one team, however, it was a time of trauma and tension as their charge was returned to the sanctity of the pit lane where it spent an anxious 30 minutes while the mechanics beavered about its rear. The car in question was the Heyer/Redman/Heywood Jaguar, car no. 52. Was it an omen? Was the savage carnivore about to become but a tame pussy? And then there were the Hawaiian Tropic girls....

The Silk Cut machine was back on *la piste*, presumably in good health, in time for the vehicles to be moved into their grid positions pending the start. After the start to fire up their engines, Nick Nicholson's Tiga BDT looked an ominous candidate to post the first retirement as it was already smoking quite heavily.

At precisely 15H54 the black BMW pace car, with lights a-flashing, led Bob Wollek and the others away on the pace lap and the tension mounted. The crowds that amassed both sides of the Pits Straight were left with nothing to look at save each other and the band of workmen who toiled to replace the double layer of armco that represented the access point half way down the pit wall. They would finish their task just as the BMW cleared the Ford Chicane. Meanwhile, for those fortunate enough to be in the Press Box atop the Citroen Stand, there was the alternative distraction of observing a phalanx of helicopters that traced the progress of the protagonists in the summer sky: an Alouette shadowed a Nissan while neither would silhouette a skylark. Stuck followed Wollek and the Bell followed Stuck. As the BMW hove into view, the pack bayed behind it; at the very last moment the pace car swerved off and the race was on!

The two Rothmans cars accelerated hard as one as the field fanned out, the drivers ever conscious of their sponsors' needs and the television cameras besides being hyped up on the adrenalin of the moment.

Thierry Boutsen feinted to go inside Stuck and then outside him, finally deciding that discretion was the better part of valour, while respective team mates Larrauri and Schuppan took a watching brief at 170mph.

First callers in the pits were t Kouros Merce (top) the Coug Toyota and Rondeau (cent and WM (left) (KW)

It was on the other side of the track, though, that the real action was taking place for Ludwig exploded out of third spot to be alongside the pole position car by the time they reached the recently replaced armco sections in the pit wall - and the Jaka-Q car was just inches off leaving a yellow stain along the barrier as Wollek, like a true professional, left just enough room for the faster man to complete the manoeuvre - sufficient to make it possible, but not so much as to make it easy.

It was not just a matter of boost settings either, for attempting to emulate Ludwig was Derek Warwick in the XJR-6, but the Frenchman managed to hold him off so that by the time they reached the Esses, it was Klaus Ludwig from Wollek and Warwick, Boutsen, Stuck and Heyer.

Down the Mulsanne for the first time and Boutsen was well beaten for pace by the German pair while Warwick was sufficiently close to Wollek to outbrake him into the corner at the end. So now it

was Ludwig from the Jaguar, then the Rothmans pair followed by the second Jaguar, then Larrauri and Schuppan led the Kouros duo who led the rest.

Hans Heyer was really motivated and split the works Porsches by the time they reached Virage Porsche to finalise the top 10 order by the end of lap one. The next three positions were the province of a determined Gartner, Follmer and Baldi followed by the third Silk Cut entry which had apparently been metamorphosed from a cat into a tortoise by Tom Walkinshaw's magic spell.

Meanwhile the gremlins were out for unlucky 13, the Cougar, who lost a door first time down the Mulsanne and nearly 20 minutes rectifying the problem only to do just three more laps before it happened again. The second stop was for over four hours so by the time it was repaired, France's best hope was some 73 laps behind the leaders.

Another to stop first time round was the

Argo with Martin Birrane at the wheel, the Zakspeed engine confirming Schanche's worst fears, and leaving the London estate agent to reflect that he might have been better off in his old Ford C100 instead. Just avoiding the wooden spoon of posting the first retirement was a Tiga BDT, not the Nicholson car as feared, but the sister machine of David Andrews when the driveshafts gave up the ghost.

In the C2 category, Stanley Dickens took class honours from the Fiero first time around with Del Bello and Haldi next up in their Rondeau and WM respectively, followed at a distance by the URD, the Sauber and all. Coming on strong were David Leslie in the Ecosse and Evan Clements aboard the ADA car who, by the end of the first hour, would be fourth and fifth in class behind the Rondeau. By that time, the Spice team had stamped their authority on proceedings and opened a gap on the works Gebhardt. It was all looking good for 'Gordy'.

The Cougar (above) after having had its door repaired in the opening stages of the race. (DC)

Another to stop first time round was the Argo with Martin Birrane at the wheel. (DC)

Third in its second race in 1980, the Rondeau M379 could manage no better than 18th in 1986. (DC). Three rear views shot (below). (GD)

The Warwick/Cheever/Schlesser Jaguar reached 2nd place before its demise. (DC)
The ill-fated Kremer Porsche of Jo Gartner. (DC)

It was also looking good for Heyer as he challenged Wollek when they went down to the Mulsanne Kink for the second time, actually getting alongside briefly, but by the time they reached the corner, the Frenchman was clear and Hans Stuck had slipped through on the inside to claim fourth. Hans was now on the move and next time past the Hunaudieres headed his team mate as the pair duly closed on the Jaguar. The World Champion was up to second by the end of the next lap when he slipped past Warwick at Virage Ford while Boutsen surrendered his place to Schuppan in an identical manoeuvre at the same spot a few seconds later. Stuck reeled in the yellow car and produced what would stand as his car's fastest race lap on lap seven, being rewarded for his efforts by blasting ahead of Ludwig as they passed the pits to start lap eight.

Klaus was not finished however, oh no, and was back in front by the end of the tour, staying there until the first pit stops which occured about 10 minutes short of the hour. During that initial hour, Follmer wiped off the tail of the second Joest car and lost a lap while obtaining a replacement while both Kouros Saubers had suffered setbacks that would eventually lead to their early demise. All that frantic activity, with more place changes amongst the leading contenders than at the average Grand Prix, and there were another 23 hours to go! Breathless stuff.!

A pattern was already starting to emerge and it clearly showed that Porsche no. 7 and the two conventional Rothmans cars had an edge on the field in terms of outright performance as they gradually drew away from their pursuers of whom the two leading XJR-6s, and a pair of Brun machines, looked like the only possible threats over the distance.

The additional cars of each of these teams formed the next group with th Kenwood, Danone and Liqui-Mo examples making up the numbers fro whom the minor placings were likely to t decreed by the Fates.

As Derek Bell had said, thoug "Things go wrong in 24 hours so who ca say?"

It was going wrong for 'Gordy' after ju 75 minutes, the Fiero losing four laps whe the practice maladies with the clutch re appeared, so returning the class lead to th factory Gebhardt. Things were not goir right for the other Gebhardt when To Dodd-Noble had a rear offside Avon ty tear apart at about the two hour mark, b he managed to avoid hitting anything an slowly trundled the now not-so-pretty 84 back to the pits. As he did so he glide behind the catch-fencing at the Virag Ford and was subsequently docked a lap t the stewards for not completing the la properly.

Tom Dodd-Noble brings the hobbled ADA Gebhardt back to the pits but was later docked a lap for going behind the catch-fencing at the Virage Ford. (KW)

After Porsche No. 7 and the two conventional Rothmans cars it was the two Brun machines (above and left) that looked like the only possible threat to the Jaguars over the distance. (KW)

Joest Porsche No. 7 easily outpaced its sister car, No. 8, in the early stages of the race (below left) while the ADA Gebhardt was moving out of contention for the class lead after its stop for tyres. (WK)

The Jaguar (below) easily outpaced the Mercedes. (WK)

Derek Bell's words of wisdom seemed anxious to haunt him when amongst the sudden flurry of dramas that preceded sunset, the first front runner to retire was from his own team when the PDK car broke its gearbox after less than three hours. Both Schuppan and Olsen had praised the technology as being the way of the future, but the future was not here yet, and while the amiable Aussie reverted to the way of the present, by being drafted into the Mass/Wollek car, the American coming-man was left to ponder his future alone.

Silk Cut 3 - Rothmans 2. Any pleasure the TWR people may have gleaned from their adversary's downfall was quickly dispersed when Jaguar no. 52 went missing from the charts soon afterwards. The fuel readout had indicated sufficient essence for another two laps, but the tank was apparently dry so what was otherwise a perfectly healthy racing car spent the remainder of the event as an ornament at Indianapolis Corner.

It was particularly galling on a number of accounts, one being that it had all the hallmarks of the problems they had encountered at Monza which prevented a potentially good result there and could now hang like the Sword of Damocles over the remaining two Jaguars here. Another sadness was the fact that the excellent Heyer, in his second stint, had got himself to the head of Jaguar's 'in-house' fight and while engaged in a titanic struggle with Barilla, who now piloted the Taka-Q car, had managed to stave off the leader and set the team's fastest race lap on the very round before the V12 spluttered to a halt. Silk Cut 2 - Rothmans 2.

Another calamity for one of the major forces was that of the second Joest entry. The 'Spirit of America' team had been making steady progress after the earlier accident that befell Follmer, and the Californian was ready and waiting to take over on his second stint, when Miller failed to appear on schedule. The tall, straight-backed man stood silently waiting, his open-faced helmet betraying his concern. From the depth of the pits 'dugout' came a crackle of a voice over the radio link and all the team's major personnel, including George, huddled around the receiver trying to make sense of the voice from afar. It was as if they were enacting a scene from a Sci-Fi movie, establishing contact with a spacecraft out there somewhere in the heavens. In reality the projectile was very much Earthbound and just a couple of miles down the road! It transpired that the 956 had stopped due to fuel problems but the driver adamant that there was some left aboard.

The Liqui-Moly car was making up the numbers in the race but still managed to finish in the top ten. (DC)

Slowly and methodically the team relayed instructions to the pilot, sorry driver, to check out the various components of the fuel system, but with no success. Time ticked by and laps were being lost, laps that could prove vital come Sunday afternoon. Finally it was discovered that Miller had not switched to the auxiliary supply and once done, he limped home where car no. 8 took on a full 99 litres before Follmer blasted off into the unknown.

One known quantity, however, was the fact that the longer the race went on, the more it became a contest between the two blue cars and the one yellow car. They were putting more and more distance between themselves and the rest, so try as they might, it was going to need some good fortune to smile upon the Jaguars if they were to win. All they could do was to keep up the pressure and await developments. At least it did not look as if it was going to rain so somebody must have been on their side. Whoever it was keeping a weather eye on the Jaguars was certainly no friend of Porsche 961 for in the warm and dry conditions, it could manage no better than a midfield placing as night approached.

The setting Sun also heralded the symbolic veil over the efforts of two contenders from the Land of the Rising Sun when, firstly, the Katayama Mazda had transmission failure then the Nissan R86V suffered engine problems which were explained as being the thrust washer allowing the crankshaft to rattle backwards and forewards! To appease Japanese honour the Tom's/Leyton House Toyota would also be out before midnight to make it one apiece.

Another in trouble was Brun Motorsport who lost the patron's car due to a dropped valve and the Blanchet Locatop example within half an hour of each other. Thierry Boutsen had hit the concrete wall at the chicane while experiencing severe tyre problems. Yvon had preceded him into the barrier at the same spot with the works Gebhardt not long before. This left the ever steady Ecosse V6 of Messrs Mallock, Wilds and Leslie out in front of C2 just half a lap ahead of the hard charging Fiero. Here they were, two entirely different approaches attempting to achieve the required result, the two class entries in the category. The Pontiac DFL equipe's chances again took a severe jolt when it lost the clutch completely and with it over two-and-a-half hours while a replacement was fitted. It would be on the stroke of midnight that Mr Spice returned to the track, to live to fight another day.

Petery in the old Ecosse DFV. Their points for 16th place would prove crucial at the end of the se (DC)

Come the witching hour and the clock ticked on. The statistics of the moment showed the Bell/Holbert/Stuck machine but 4.3 seconds ahead of the Taka-Q while slowly, inexorably they began to drop the second Rothmans machine. The crowd of three was becoming a company of two. Round and round they went, time after time, and in the cool night air they turned up the heat. Through the darkness they drove often only a few scant seconds apart, sometimes less, with the pole position car just a little back, ready and waiting. The expertise of Larrauri had got the surviving Brun car, with it's Fortuna cigarettes

livery, up with the Silk Cut XJR-6s wh had the 'saloon' car leading the 'star' car a result of more niggling problems fe both. Danone, Kenwood and the 'Spirit America' machines were all now comir into the frame and much earlier tha predicted due to the misfortunes of other The Ecosse still led C2, now by four lap from the steady Rondeau 102 with the UR clear of the repaired ADA Gebhardt looking pretty again! Richard Cleare March had closed within two laps of th remaining Mazda while the 961 and the M just kept trucking on doing battle wit nobody but themselves.

Night-time racing at the Sarthe circuit. The time and place when legends are made. (GD)

e Tom's Toyota (above) was never really in the hunt and retired after seven hours. (DC). Despite the comparatively lumbering look of the
rsche 961 (below), it ended the race in the 7th position, 6 places ahead of the Grand/Goudchaux/Menant Rondeau M482. (GD)

Overleaf: it was during the hours of darkness, while designer Tony Southgate catnapped (inset) (KW) that the second Jaguar, car No. 53,
succumbed to failure; this time due a driveshaft giving way. The Alba was also doomed to retire during the night as well. (GD)

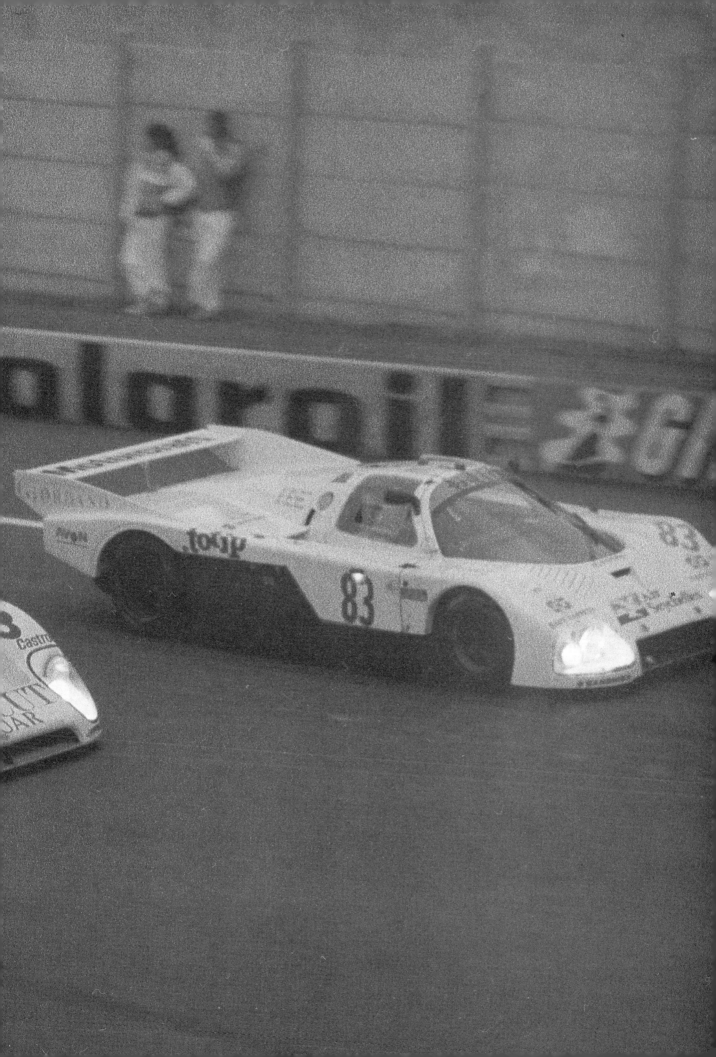

While the carnival continues, the hard work goes on, but not for much longer on the Taka-Q Porsche, as moments later the hope for a third consecutive victory was dashed by a faulty engine. (KW/DC)

Opposite: Night stop for Win Percy. (KW)

Le Mans has atmosphere twenty-four hours a day but it is those few hours of darkness that really make it special. As the carnival takes over and the beer begins to flow the circuit takes on an ethereal quality with the red and white lights like tracer bullets in the night. While cars flash past at hundreds of miles per hour in a blur of light and sound and speed, enthusiasts slumber but a few feet away. Of what do they dream? The hardy ones, however, can be seen standing defiantly against the moonlit backdrop determined not to miss a morsel, a second of it. They talk of having made it out to the Mulsanne as if it were an expedition to compare with the likes of Columbus or Magellan or Livingstone. What do they see when they get there? Probably only the blaze of indistinguishable lights. However they also get the aura and soul of Le Mans for where else can you see a car doing about 200 mph on a public road at night? The day of AC Cobras on the M.1 are long gone - and there are too many cones these days anyway! Better though is the vision away from the straight and narrow, for racing cars, unlike dragsters, look much more spectacular through a curve or a bend. To stand around the Esses and out along to Tertre Rouge is a wholly more satisfying experience. The reflections of light beneath the Dunlop Bridge tell you they're

on their way, then it's down past the fairground and through the left-right sweep of the Esses where carefully chosen positions allow one to see them from almost any angle. Then it's up to Tertre Rouge, hard on the brakes, and as the headlamps pick out the tall stark trees, it's up through the gearbox and away. Super stuff!

The hours of darkness were not the stuff that legends were made of for the C1 Secateva or the second Mazda, both falling victims to the night. The loss of the second rotary car meant that Richard Cleare was now alone in the GTP category so the class would be his if only he could keep going. Another lonesome soul was the Grand Prix Jaguar after a driveshaft gave way on Win Percy's mount with the saloon ace two laps ahead of its nominal team leader. Until that point things had gone remarkably well for the Silk Cut tortoise but with car no. 51 now some seven laps behind the fantastic dice for the lead, it would need all the pace the aces could muster if they were to catch and overtake the Porsches ahead to win Le Mans - unless, that was, the progress of Stuttgart's finest was impaired.

And impaired it was when, with 11 hours to go, Jochen Mass discovered oil at the Porsche Curves and his 962 went straight on. Immediately in his path was Mike Wilds in the class leading Ecosse who

had proceeded him into the boonies.

Mike explained later: "I hit a patch oil coming down through the Porsc Curves and spun, the next car comi down was Jochen Mass. I'd just finish my spin and Jochen lost it on the oil a collected my car as well." Flags? "N nothing, the first thing I knew about the was when I was going backwards. At nig you just cannot see it," and continued was about the same time that Jo had his accident so the pace car was out, the gu repaired the car in 45 minutes and we st got out in the lead of C2."

The former German merchant sail had swiped the nose off the Ecosse, b had done far more damage to his ov craft; sufficient in fact to leave it high a dry, beached against the barrier.

The oil slick was, reputedly, caused the gearbox of the Kenwood Kremer c losing its contents and has been suggeste as a contributory factor to the accident th befell Gartner moments later. The popul Austrian was about half an hour into h stint and attempting to make up time aft a variety of problems had delayed the c earlier on. Now into eighth place an rapidly closing on the 'Spirit of Americ machine that held the position above, t black machine suddenly veered into t barriers on the left, flipped over, sl across the track and came to rest in flam on the right hand side of the course. A fe hundred metres later and the dreadf scene would have been enacted in full vie of the mass of enthusiasts that mill around the famous Hunaudier Restaurant. Gartner was apparently dea even before the remains of the 962 came rest. The pace cars were immediately se out while the emergency services replace the damaged armco and cleared away t carnage. The fact that they were to rema in position for two and a half hours is son reflection on the severity of the acciden

Many in the pitlane were aware Gartner's fate within a short time of occurence, but it was not until 04H24 th the public was informed. A solem message in French did not ne translation, but then came the Englis commentator advising: "Ladies an gentlemen, we regret to announce...."

In the cool, dark night there wa unusually, a moment of peace as t contestants paid silent tribute to one their own. Then over the tannoy came t haunting, if inappropriate, strains of t Jennifer Rush pop song 'The Power Love', the show must go on. A group about a dozen cars passed in single fil close rank formation behind a pace ca their speed still slowed, their noise st muted as if in respect, each knowing t race must go on.

Jochen Mass moments after his accident at the Porsche Curves. (KW)

he Kenwood Kremer car at dusk. It was not to see the night out. (GD)

ans Stuck slips behind the steering wheel of car No. 1. (GD)

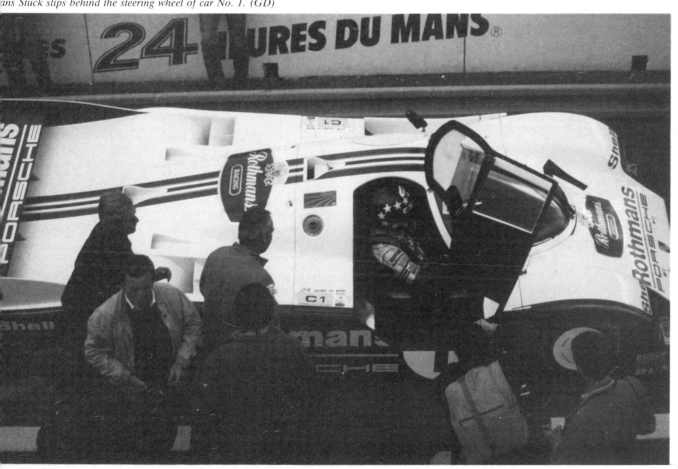

6 o'clock in the morning, both cars still out on the circuit, so a chance for the Ecosse man to catch up. (KW). The Lassig/Ballabio/Wood 956 comes in for a 'brush and wash up' before resuming the race and its way to 5th place. (KW). The magnificent Rothmans Porsche 962 with Hans Stuck at the wheel, on its way to victory. (DC)

The Secateva WM P85 chases the Gordon Spice Pontiac Fiero while on its way to 12th place and 3rd C2 car home. (DC)

The Porsche 961 (below left) in the pits during a refuelling stop. Unfortunately for the team, the rain stayed away, otherwise it would have done better than its final 7th placed spot. (KW). The Nissan R85V (below right) of Hasemi/Wada/Weaver comes into the pits for refuelling on its way to a disappointing 16th place. (KW)

As the final notes of the song drifted away into the night another group of similarly controlled contestants came by to start yet another lap behind one of the BMWs. One of their number broke ranks and cruised up the sliproad to stop at the first pit. It was the Ludwig car.

The well drilled Joest mechanics were immediately into action as every moment was precious because, with the aid of the pace car, the Bell/Stuck/Holbert machine had closed to within four seconds of the wonderful yellow racer. With 12 hours gone and 12 hours to go, it was a virtual stalemate, honours even with the lead having changed about a dozen times as the gladiators sought to break each other.

Reinhold Joest stood by, proud and aloof, watching proceedings when after what was probably only a few seconds the door swung open and the man, whose three bands of blue on his helmet seem to represent a trio of wins at the Sarthe, stalked in the glare of the brightly lit 'dugout'. A brief conversation ensued, the strain of the occasion and the lateness of the hour etched into every face. Then a mechanic drew an index finger across his

neck as if to cut this throat: the Taka-Q car was out and the dream of a third successive win for chassis 117 was over. In the space of five minutes all the enjoyment and most of the interest in Le Mans '86 had gone.

As the Joest personnel prepared to concentrate all their efforts on the surviving 'Star Spangled Banner' entry that was now flying the flag in fifth place it was ironic to think that the Taka-Q model itself, so swift and so economical, had succumbed to the pressures of its time in purgatory behind the pace car. It could race fast but it could not run slow. The supposed magic microchip in the engine's electronic brain had given the works Porsches a few headaches in its time, but on this occasion, it was the Joest team that lost its marbles.

This all had a dramatic effect on the race and by the time the pace car withdrew the remaining Rothmans car had a massive nine lap lead from the Brun Fortuna example with the Jaguar but a minute further in arrears, but well clear of the JFR Danone 956. Further back, good runs from the 936 and 961, both now in the top 10, maintained superiority for the nor-

Ludwig (above) in the Joest 'dugout' moments after the car has retired. (KW). The Brun Fortuna car (below) was the main beneficiary of the retirement as it now moved up to 2nd place. (DC)

Porsche No. 1 on its way to the marque's 11th victory. (WK)

alian team that features a black prancing orse on a yellow background as part of its mblem. Last year the Stuttgart concern loved ahead of the Scuderia in terms of lost overall wins at the world's greatest ce and with only the XJR-6 and the ninth laced Dome Toyota of those within 25 ps of the leader, who did not hail from le Weissach facility, it was looking nlikely that anybody was going to stop lem increase their lead in the listing.

While the likes of the Toyota and the lickey Mouse 956 - reputably the oldest xample still racing - continued to make rogress up the leaderboard, the arrival of new dawn did not herald new joys for thers. It was now David Leslie's turn to lffer drama with the Ecosse when a tyre urst on Mulsanne and he subsequently lade three stops en route back to the pits replenish the damaged radiator with life ving water. Unfortunately his only eward was to be disqualified for taking on

fluids outside the pits area, but the team can well be pleased by their efforts and especially by the reliability of John Dunn's V6.

The ADA Gebhardt was now clear in the class, its closest rival being the reliable Castrol URD while the Fiero was running superbly, but having lost too much time to be of any threat to anything save the lap record. Ray Bellm finally left it at 3m36.60. The quality of the challenge can be measured in the fact that this time was 10.1 seconds below the lap record time set by David Leslie last year and nearly four seconds inside its own practice best for this year's event. For sure the Fiero and the new Ecosse are destined to have a worthy battle with the likes of the Gebhardts there, awaiting and awatching, ready to step into the breach.

Schlesser had been going like a bullet in his endeavours to pull clear of Brun car no. 17, when the team decided to step up the

pressure on the leader. As the crowds regathered around breakfast time, the TWR machine was reeling in the easily paced Rothmans at a rate of about 10 seconds a lap, but with a lead of eight tours, over 60 miles, Norbert Singer and Co. were not yet ready to be anxious about stepping up their own pace and with the extra rations of fuel gleaned from the pace car period, there was always the opportunity of just turning up the wick if it should prove necessary. The Number One car in number one position was running faultlessly and unlikely to be caught by anyone unless the gremlins chose otherwise.

The Jaguar people must have mislaid their lucky black cats for the gremlins did choose otherwise - Silk Cut 51. There is, perhaps, some higher morality in the fact that Jaguar's bid was finally thwarted by the very same fate that befell the Ecosse, a name with which it is irrevocably linked.

lthough the Jaguar was reeling in the leading Porsches, a tyre explosion on the Mulsanne Straight spelled the end of the race for car No. 51. (WK)

Winnter Hans Stuck, Al Holbert and Derek Bell. Opposite: An Al Holbert/Hans Stuck driver change in the leading Porsche. (KW)

Before the end of the 17th hour, Jean-Louis had a massive moment when a tyre exploded on the Mulsanne at well over 200mph, the carcass acting like a flail as it ripped through fragile bodywork and, more importantly, damaging the suspension sufficiently to make it *hors de combat*.

That was it, the Jaguar dream had disappeared in that very instant that rubber met metal on the stretch of track that flanks the local golf club. Jaguar 0 - Rothmans 1. Silk Cut had scored a triple bogey while the Porsche birdie was flying high. Jaguar had failed in their quest, fair enough, but they had put up one hell of a fight, undoubtedly learned a lot and are already being spoken of as winners next year. In 1987, there will not be any Rothmans, any works team apparently - but there will possibly be the yellow peril from Abtsteinach....

The demise of the last Jaguar was, in many eyes, the last significant occurence of the race, but although most competitors were now well spread out, there was some honour to be gained by trying to improve, or just maintain, one's position.

John Fitzpatrick was well aware that his Danone car was being dropped by the battle-scarred Fortuna 962 which had now re-inherited second place while being caught rapidly by the fourth placed Joest no. 8, but was powerless to intercede due to suspension problems. The Americans were ahead in time for elevenses and got within four and a half laps of Larrauri by the close. How they must have rued the down time when Miller was stranded on the track so many hours before.

The second JFR entry, the Elkron liveried example for Alliot and partners, was also in trouble and slipped three places to 10th by the end, but they were luckier than the Toyota whose engine roasted itself just over an hour from the flag.

The 936, Jens Winther and the Ecosse DFL all had good reason to be pleased with their efforts while the Nissan people were probably satisfied to be the only Japanese finisher on a weekend that promised so much, delivered so little and will haunt the memory of so many.

The Bardon struggled to the end after looking to post an early retirement when it stopped out on the circuit on Saturday evening while the BMW crawled home, mobile but unclassified. Through all this came the unlucky Spice crew and the Cougar who may well have been good enough for sixth had not it lost so much time with the door problems. Why do so many cars persistently suffer so and spoil such potentially good results for such a stupid problem?

The fourth placed Joest car. (DC)

The 10th placed JFR 956. (DC)

The Bardon struggled to the end, but was unclassified. (KW)

The Schuster Porsche 936CJ finished a good 6th. (DC)

…DA won the C2 class and was the only non Porsche in the top 10. (GD)

…he 961 came home 7th and the Cougar 18th. (GD)

ADA got their reward for many years of honest toil to notch up the C2 class and the only non Porsche in the top 10 which included the 961 in seventh. The four-wheeled drive machine had lost time with a number of difficulties but despite being 50 laps adrift of its illustrious cousin by the end proved the basic soundness of the enterprise by finishing first time out.

Derek Bell reeled off the last hour in the leading Rothmans 962, a position they both knew so well, to record a fine win - his fourth. For Al Holbert it was much less traumatic than 1983 when he had to fend off a hard-charging Bell, in an ailing machine, to score his first win. For Hans Stuck it was a just reward to the man who has done so much to make motor racing a pleasure and currently could be claimed to be the fastest in Group C these days.

The finish saw the traditional and chaotic invasion of the circuit that preceded a balcony scene that bore no resemblance to similar placements to either Buckingham Palace or Romeo and Juliet. One would have been forgiven for thinking 'Jaguar, Jaguar, wherefore art thou, Jaguar' but the Silk Cut team had already left their answer for their fans. Sprayed defiantly on the boards that fronted their pits were the statements 'Thanks for Coming' and 'We'll be Back.'

That was tomorrow, however, while today belonged to the men from Rothmans Porsche Number 1. Initially only Stuck and Holbert could be seen while everyone, particularly the still vocal British, awaited the man who had brought the car home and was now having more problems with getting through the crowds of well-wishers than he had ever experienced with the race traffic. When he finally appeared, the crowd erupted into a crescendo of noise every bit as warm and loud as that which greeted the Jaguar drivers during yesterday's parades. Oh, how they cheered Derek Bell at Le Mans this year.

The 24 hour man

Derek Bell

<u>The</u> 24 hour man, four times winner of the Le Mans 24 hour race. Winning in 1975, 1981, 1982 and in 1986 in a Porsche 962C, partnered by Hans Stuck and Al Holbert, he became the first British driver to win Le Mans four times. Le Mans − 24 hours of concentrated teamwork, attention to detail and precise rapid decisions. Organisation of the highest calibre is essential to compete in this ultimate long distance race. Derek Bell twice World Sports Car Champion has a wide range of talent as a racing driver, but he is also a team man − and as such wears the Autoglass logo proudly on his race overalls, allying himself to an organisation dedicated to all the principals of teamwork that he knows are so vital for success.

The 24 hour service

Autoglass

Autoglass are on hand, around the clock, when motorists of Britain break <u>any</u> glass in their vehicle. The service that is recommended by Motor Insurers and the AA to members, moves into top gear when drivers of cars, coaches, trucks or heavy plant dial direct free on 0800 36 36 36. A centrally controlled network of bases ensure fast and efficient service, nationwide.

Autoglass are proud of their track record − whether the glass is fitted in a base or, in an emergency, on the road by one of their fleet in the distinctive red and gold livery that is the mark of an organisation working day and night to maintain its lead in automotive glass replacement.

AUTOGLAS

Victory for car No. 1 as it crosses the finishing line. (KW)

Hans Stuck, Derek Bell and Al Holbert receive the cheers from the crowd on the victory podium. (KW)

PER ARNAGE AD ASTRA

by
The Prancing Tortoise

More and more British enthusiasts seem to be attending the event that was once described as 'a British motor race held in France.' This year, with the additional interest created by the Jaguars of the TWR Squadron, it was estimated that their numbers exceeded 30,000 - a staggering 30% of the paying public. It is quite extra-ordinary how many of them make a full week of it thereby enjoying scrutineering, practice/qualifying and the whole atmosphere of the build up to 4 o'clock Saturday afternoon. The great majority of the early arrivals have the benefit of their own transport and one of the favourite ways to absorb some of the atmosphere is to go cruising on the road out of town towards Tours, the RN 138.

The six kilometre section of road that is the focus of their attentions is no more remarkable than any other stretch of the highway that originates at Rouen, except for the fact that on a few days each year someone casts a magic spell over it and it becomes the epitome of all the dramas and danger, all the speed and splendour of *Les Vingt Quatre Heures du Mans:* the Mulsanne Straight. A small village famous for just being there: Mulsanne - the very name is evocative. There may be other claimants to the title of most famous track in the world, but there can be no denying that this is the most famous portion of any track anywhere. Why, the 'Bentley Boys' even named a car after it!

The cruisers can join in at Tertre Rouge (Red Hill to you and me) and must be immediately struck by the comparative narrowness of the road surface. It is really a two lane highway so overtaking in a road car at road speeds can be a precarious experience, so depite the fact that during the race everyone is travelling in the same direction (hopefully!) the extra width of the contenders, their incredible speeds and the way that they are thrown about by the humps and bumps must make such manoeuvres very daunting indeed. There are wide gravel areas down both sides of 'the strip' but to get a couple of wheels onto the loose at 200mph cannot help the pulse rate! There is a mixture of industrial and domestic buildings flanking the road, both large and small, moderate and expensive. One wonders if living on the Mulsanne Straight constitutes a good reason for a rate rebate?

The Hunaudieres bar/restaurant/hotel complex is amongst the buildings nearly half way down - the very same establishment to which the Porsche people traditionally retire after the race. This is a good vantage point to watch fellow cruisers from Aston Martin to VW Camper, 'rep' Sierra to D-type replica all savouring the delights of doing the Mulsanne. Another good reason to stop at this point lies opposite where a discreet sign directs you up a dirt track to the local horse racing circuit - and you thought there was only one track at Le Mans! 400 metres away, in the days when automobiles were in their infancy and aeroplanes even more so, Wilbur Wright made his first ever flight in Europe from this very spot. The occasion is marked by a granite plinth and it is interesting to note that amongst the organisers of this historic feat was the fledgling A.C.O - the same club that arranges the 24 Hours. Further links with aviation occured during World War 2 when the Luftwaffe, besides using their main base adjacent to the pits straight, used the Mulsanne as a runway! When they said they were flying, they really meant it!

The other major feature of the Mulsanne Straight is the infamous Kink. Participants are expected to hurtle through the right-hand 'twitch' without lifting and rely on good marshalling to warn of dangers ahead. I remember listening to Michel Savage once recalling an occasion when, flat out, there was an almighty bang. For a split second, which undoubtedly must have seemed like an eternity, he did not know what had happened. Was it the engine? Perhaps a tyre? Maybe the suspension had broken? Had the bodywork gone taking with it the car's stability? All of these possibilities, and more, rushed through his head: the only definite factor being that if something drastic had happened he would be powerless to control the maelstrom of destruction that would soon follow. Luckily for him it was only that a perspex side window had blown out under a build up of air pressure!

At the end of the road is the revised Mulsanne Corner which now boasts a roundabout where the crossroads used to be. The racers do not actually enter the roundabout, but take a slip road to the right. Most of the Mulsanne cruisers tend to do a loop of the roundabout and head back up the RN 138 - usually as far as the Hunaudieres.

The real, intrepid enthusiast is recommended to turn down past the signalling area onto the CD 140. How the driver of a car whose signalling area is close to the corner is expected to read the instructions while trying to negotiate the bend at full chuff is beyond me - and that's only during a nice sunny day. As for rain or darkness etc! Or both! There's more to this driving game than lots of wellie!

The right turn adroitly accomplished - if not you'll be in the 'kitty litter' - it is then a straight two kilometre blast towards Indianapolis. The smoother road surface on this section must be a welcome relief to the racers after the rigours of the Mulsanne. Dipping slightly at the end there is a right hand curve into the corner which is heavily cambered to the le thereby giving the enthusiast full value sensation as, one presumes, he/she already travelling on the right hand side the road! There then follows a short das to the very tight right hander at Arna before the long drag up to the Porsch Curve where, as at Tertre Rouge, th access is blocked except during ra activity. To get this far has meant coveri two thirds of the course - the equivalent Brands Hatch and Silverstone.

This, however, need not be the end the matter. From the Porsche Curve o can clearly see the imposing grandstan lining the pits straight. Taking the roa towards them will immediately transpo you back nearly two decades along section of track that was used up un 1971. A couple of fast, sweeping curves a bordered by a small collection homesteads, one of which tends to obscu the view along the road. It is a dra unremarkable building in dirty white: t true, the real, Maison Blanche. Sto awhile and savour the atmosphere. The are wide grassy run-off areas wi forbidding high banks and ominous de ditches. A concrete wall affronting o property still bears the inscriptic 'TOTAL' in faded red paint, some s times or so along its length like son Neanderthal masterpiece. The 12km. pc still stands by the roadside as a permane memorial to those who passed this w with no time read it. Listen and you m hear a D-type howling in the wind, t thunder of a 'Blower Bentley' st reverberating around the brickwork or t scream of a P4 echoing through a piqu fence. Did 917s really do battle over th very surface?

So next time you go to Le Mans, early. Cruise down the Mulsanne a absorb its awesome reputation. Gli through Indianapolis and Arnage to enj a couple of classic bends. The impulse is do it quickly, but there is no need to rus the gendarmes abound in their little bl R4s - on the spot speeding fines can 900FF a time - while an abundance lorries suggests lots to thwart would- heroes. There is no need to follow t example of the driver of a certain whi Astra van who is probably still dining o on the tale of being the fastest ev Vauxhall around 'Indy' and almost too the bristles off the brush held by the m painting the rouge et blanc rumble strips he went. Who does he think he is anywa No, it is far better to take it slowly a enjoy every metre of it: there is nothing say you cannot do it more than once - a when you get to the White House, stop a look and listen.

And remember, let's be careful o there.

FORD FIESTA

he Ford Motor Company celebrated the 20th anniversary of their
st Le Mans victory in splendid, if understated, style.

They were represented at the pre-race parade of *voitures
ciennes* by a pair of GT40s, courtesy of club secretary Bryan
'ingfield, namely Jean-Francis Charray's Ford France car and the
bulous FEL 1C driven on this occasion by Terry Hoyle.
:rversely they flanked, amongst other things, the striking Jaguar
J13 against which so many epic battles went unfought as a result of
negative policy by Coventry's hierarchy during the darker days of
; past. Interestingly, Bryan's own XJ13-type Ecosse is, if anything,
'en more beautiful than its inspiration.

If the Le Mans organisers could only get a dozen or so cars for
eir parade, they were totally outshone when Ford put on their
vn private shindig at Boreham a fortnight later. No less than 80
rs were presented in glorious weather befitting to such an
:casion.

The two GT40s that went to Le Mans were joined by six
rther examples including a superb roadster, licence plate GT40,
at proceeded to embarrass itself by melting its plug leads. The
'ent was actually heralded as a 'Ford - Ferrari Le Mans Day' so
ere were a whole string of prancing horses, including a pair of

Daytonas whose silver sheen offset the many shades of ubiquitous
red....Over here was a 512BB, over there a Testa Rossa, a Lusso
and a brace of 250SWBs. Green is often regarded as unlucky by the
superstitious, but to see a 250LM lined up alongside a Porsche 917K
and Peter Millward's Lola-Aston Martin, all in differing hues of the
sward, made you feel unlucky that you did not own one! Alongside
the Lola, as it awaited its turn on the track, sat a Cobra, then a D-
type and a trio of C's. There were Bentleys and Lagondas and an
Austin-Healey 3000 that was so enthusiastically driven it was not
overshadowed by anybody or anything.

Meanwhile, forlorn on a trailer, slumbered a Ford F3L as a
reminder to everyone that racing is an uncertain science. David
Piper also bought along his glorious Ferrari P2 but, sadly, it went
hors de combat very soon after taking to the track while Stoic
Racing's genuine, ex-Pedro, Gulf 917 never ventured beyond the
paddock. Circuit honours went to Martin Colvill's similarly liveried
GT40 and with the recent sad announcement that the track is to
become a gravel pit (what sacrilege) the unofficial outright lap
record will probably remain with the orange and blue machine. An
appropriate finale.

Will Ford celebrate their coming of age, and if so, where?

WHAT HAPPENED NEXT

It would be a full four months before the Sports-Prototype World Championship came to an exciting finish in Japan by which time there had been another five rounds. Ken Wells follows the fortunes of the competitors to the end of the trail.

It was a month before the contestants re-assembled to continue the title chase, round four of the Drivers' battle being held at the Norisring where the emotive and ominous presence of the former Nazi stadium contrasts obliquely to the mystique and aura of the Sarthe. Another contrast was that whereas the latter lasts for a full 24 hours, the famous German 'Money Race' would be over in just 67 minutes. Both count 20 points to the winner - strange things championships -and while Le Mans had three, the Nuremberg course would acclaim only one as the local organisers, for local reasons, had decided upon a single event without driver changes.

Consequently Hans Stuck had a factory Porsche, albeit in black Blaupunkt colours, which lined up in pole position alongside the white liveried Joest chassis of Klaus Ludwig from the same sponsor while Hanschen's regular partner Derek Bell sought refuge in a JFR 956.

Other new faces in new places included James Weaver putting his eastern promise behind him to replace the lamented Jo Gartner at Kremer, Indy veteran Danny Ongais under the Joest banner and Bob Wollek in the Liqui-Moly machine, but it did not prove to be a notable weekend for any of the erstwhile Rothmans trio although Hans did set a new lap record after gearbox maladies put him out of contention for overall honours when holding a slim lead over Ludwig & Co. Klaus was subsequently left to fend off his pursuers to beat an impressive Eddie Cheever by just seven seconds with Warwick third in another Jaguar well clear of Jelinski in the first of the Brun cars. The restricted nature of the event kept away most of the major C2 teams - hence no Ecosse, no Spice, no ADA - so enabling Stanley Dickens to bag top marks in the works Gebhardt by finishing well clear of Thyrring's Tiga.

All the regular runners and riders were back for the next race, at Brands Hatch, with the notable exception of the factory 962s, but Rothmans saved the day for Bell and Stuck by hiring Joest's legendary 956/117 on their behalf. The German - complete with T-shirt bearing the slogan 'I'm Stuck with Bell' - was certainly trying harder and promptly claimed pole position with his new mount, so being in an ideal position to answer the inevitable questions about discovering the secrets of its success by answering that there was no magic: just excellent drivers, superb preparation and Goodyear radials....

The first couple of hours of the race were more akin to a destruction derby as cars disappeared in all directions, the Le Mans class winners from ADA and Richard Cleare being amongst the casualties. As a consequence, the event deteriorated into mayhem, the challenge for the lead down to just three hopefuls: the Liqui-Moly and Joest-Rothmans Porsches and the Warwick/Schlesser XJR-6.

The Liqui-Moly Porsche chases the Warwick/Schlesser XJR-6 at the Brands Hatch 6 Hour race in July. (GD)

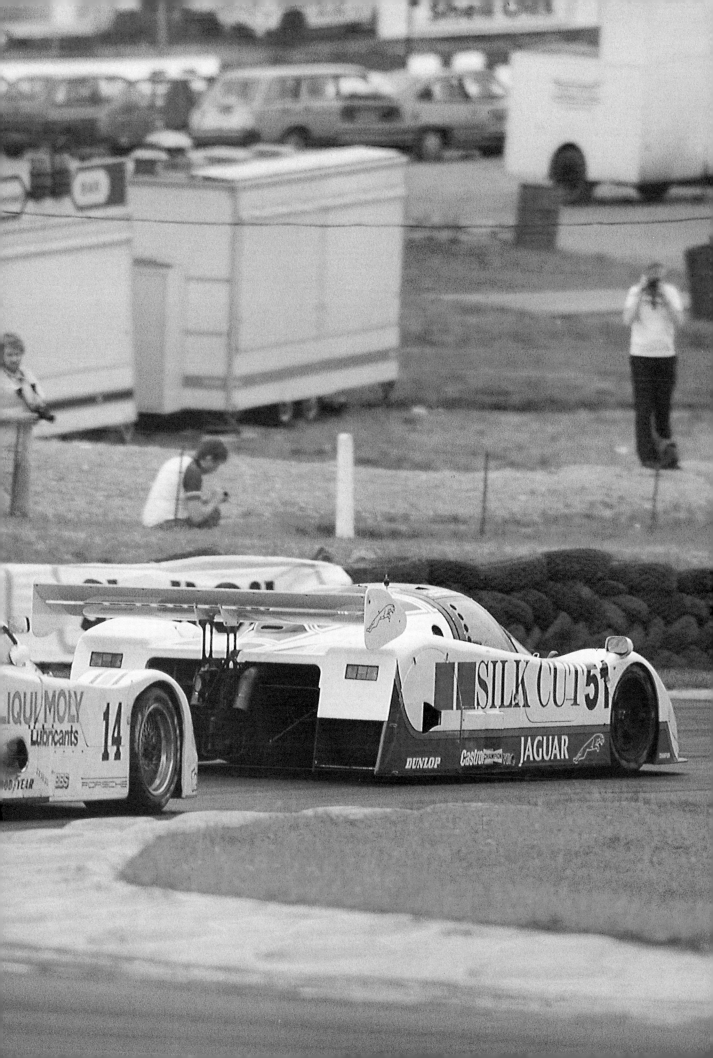

The latter two cars encountered various fuel related problems with the Jaguar being eventually pipped for third place by Boutsen and Jelinski while Stuck had to sit it out on the grid so as to avoid running out of fuel while the leaders reeled off the final laps. It was left to Wollek and Mauro Baldi to score a fine victory for Richard Lloyd's often unlucky equipe. Lady Luck also smiled on Ray Mallock too as he and David Leslie shrugged off the misfortunes of Silverstone and Le Mans to win handsomely the C2 class by a massive margin from the Kelmar Tiga and the Spice Fiero.

If the Brands' result was a disappointment to the pre-race favourites from TWR then it paled into insignificance in Jerez where at the very first turn Derek Warwick drove into Brancatelli leaving Cheever no option but to hit the Italian's car! In the most celebrated contretemps of the season, one moment of tomfoolery - much to the digress of Mr W - had put the Big Cat into the kitty litter and as Silk Cut's unofficial team leader dug furiously to extricate himself from the factual sandtrap and proverbial glasshouse, he probably did not have time to recall his earlier vociferous comments about the driving of others. He should not a stone thrower be...

This escapade left the pair of locally supported Brun machines well clear with the JFR-Danone third for a while before brake problems stopped its progress. The chastened Warwick proceeded to chase them, making haste while the sun shone, as did his new partner, Jan Lammers, while another TWR 'old boy' from the class of '85, Martin Brundle, failed to get a drive as the car he was to share with Cheever did not have any after a shaft broke; the same failure eliminating the third Jaguar very early on. So the two Fortuna backed cars ran out easy winners with Larrauri and Pareja going one better than at Le Mans to head home Jelinski and proud team patron Walter Brun. The man who had coined a living from slot machines had pulled off a double jackpot while the high profile Jaguar boys, racing for the Silk Cut Trophy no less, were left with just two lemons and a raspberry as the surviving XJR-6 could manage no better than third when defeat was snatched from the jaws of victory....

Fourth home was the Obermaier-Topolino 956 after yet another consistent run and next was the Spice/Bellm pairing comfortably ahead of the ADA and Kelmar concerns, the Tiga passing the Unlucky Strike Argo on the very last lap when a blocked fuel filter stopped its Zakspeed engine.

Three weeks later it was the third round of the teams' paper chase at the Nürburgring where the strains of 'We are off to Sunny Spain, Viva Espana' were drowned by 'Stormy Weather' at the soulless Eifel circuit, while the Gods still refused to smile on Mr Warwick as he severely damaged an XJR-6 on Friday after clipping a kerb and clouting the armco. What with the dramas with the Brabham, it never rains but it pours...

The TWR effort was thus reduced to two cars, but the race was initially a battle between the works Rothmans Porsche and Kouros Mercedes outfits - both returning to the fray for the first time since Le Mans - along with Boutsen in the Jagermeister 962. The race was stopped, however, after 22 laps due to a number of accidents and incidents which the pace car seemed to exacerbate as it picked up the midfield runners while others continued at unabated pace into the wall of spray.

The worst repercussion of the ensuing tangles was when Hans Stuck, not knowing that the race was under a spell of caution, hit the rear of team mate Jochen Mass' 962, wrecking both, before passing between the pace car and the head of its queue to strike a glancing blow on Thackwell's blue Sauber. When the race was eventually restarted some hours later, it was with a depleted grid as the Brun, Kremer and Joest teams were withdrawn in protest at the organisers' handling of the crisis which they had certainly managed to turn into a drama while neither Rothmans' car would see the light of day again. So it was left to be a straight fight between Thackwell and the veteran Pescarolo for Kouros against Warwick and Lammers in the Jaguar. Gradually, remorselessly, the British car opened up an advantage, but never was it more than a minute as the rain finally eased thereby allowing Baldi and Klaus Niedzwiedz in Richard Lloyd's Porsche to give chase after being delayed earlier by wiper motor problems. Then with less than 30 laps to go, an oil pipe broke on the V-12 so handing victory by two laps to the three-pointed star. It was Mercedes' first major track success since the days of Fangio and was not only a tremendous fillip to the team after the calamity of the Sarthe, but a welcome boost of variety to the whole Group C scene.

If variety was the spice of life now in C1, it certainly was not helping 'Gordy' for he and Ray Bellm could not manage better than third in the C2 class although even that must be regarded as somewhat fortuitous as the Fiero had been involved in one of the collisions that had caused the initial stoppage then had taken advantage of the break to repair the damage. Ahead of the C2 champions were the factory Gebhardt and the victorious Ecosse for Mallock and rally ace Marc Duez while the category's surprise pole winner, the Argo Zakspeed, had been eliminated in the first part, a cloud's silver lining not extending to cover race day....

It was Hi Ho Silver Lining for Walter Brun though as his team gained their third consecutive pole position for the penultimate round at Spa-Francorchamps courtesy of local hero Thierry Boutsen who, with partner Jelinski, used it to good effect to dictate the race from the front. The orange Jagermeister even seemed to have the situation under control when firstly the Baldi/Weaver and then the 'BEST' Porsches had brief periods ahead of it while the Taka-Q 956 and both Silk Cats were there or thereabouts for most of the duration too. The Liqui-Moly was first to fall back as poor fuel economy hindered its progress, then the Cheever/Schiesser pairing dropped out of the battle with tyre problems although Eddie continued to charge and set a new lap record just before the end.

With a dozen laps to run it was now down to just four, the quartet being separated by less than a minute after five hours hard toil, the closeness of the contest having already marked it as something special in endurance racing terms. It was Ludwig who broke the chain as he was forced to slow with the fuel economy tenterhooks so familiar to his adversaries but not normally associated with the Joest equipe while 'Dinger' was soon instructed by his pit to do likewise in an effort to make the finish for valuable championship points, so now it was just Boutsen versus Warwick, Porsche against Jaguar, as the two Grand Prix stars went for the showdown. When Derek had passed his namesake with two laps to go he was still nearly six seconds behind Thierry, but all the way round the classic Ardennes course he was gaining, gaining so upon starting the final tour the gap was halved. Boutsen reckoned to have the measure of the Englishman for it is one thing to catch the leader but another to pass him. Then suddenly, at the Bus Stop chicane the Porsche spluttered, its fuel allowance almost spent and Derek closed some more ready to pounce as they exited La Source on the downhill run to the line. There they met the ADA Gebhardt and the Ecosse going about their legitimate business although seemingly wanting to witness the dramatic finale to this splendid race from their unique vantage point. Could Boutsen hang on or would Warwick snatch a memorable revenge victory over Brun to exorcise the ghost of Jerez? It was all down grunt and welly - and hydrocarbons. As ey both, virtually simultaneously, hit the ud pedal the Jaguar roar was *sotto voce*, s V-12 unwilling to gargle the last litres of ice and in that instant the race was ecided. Boutsen and Jelinski had won by mere eight-tenths of a second. Wow! The cal boy had made good and the coming an had arrived, great stuff.

With all the excitement of the big ague it was easy to overlook the C2s who ad been fighting out their own battles ith Mallock and Duez again coming out n top although the early sensation was rand Prix man Piercarlo Ghinzani in the echnoracing Alba who, after claiming ass pole, led the first seven laps in fine yle before being sidelined by a broken ub. The class results had a familiar sight s the Fiero and ADA took the minor acings, runner up spot being sufficient or Spice and Bellm to retain their drivers' tle while fourth home came Jens Winther his farewell appearance prior to tirememt. *Au revoir*, kind sir.

It was *sayonara* to the championship of 6 when the warriors assembled at Mount uji for the final confrontation in the land f samurai, shinto and shogun. The oyota-powered Dome driven by new otus F1 recruit Saturo Nakajima recorded e fastest time in qualifying only to have e effort nullified for being a T-car, thus emoting it to the eighth row. So pole osition was, once more, the domain of run, this time Larrauri doing the job and was double bubble for them as Jelinski ned up alongside with title holders Bell nd Stuck on row two next to Hoshino and akako in the revitalised March Nissan king local honours ahead of a whole halanx of Oriental contenders.

Initially the Brun pair led from Baldi nd Stuck with the Jaguars gradually aaking progress from their lowly grid ositions as the only normally aspirated epresentatives in a sea of turbos. It was anschen who first had that sinking feeling hen he lost a lap after clipping the C2 ardon so giving Warwick, who needed a inimum of second place to have any pportunity of snatching the drivers' title, e first inkling of hope. Hope it was too at Rothmans would need - with Holbert nd Pescarolo replacing the IMSA bound lass and Wollek - as five years reliability nd good fortune deserted them with either destined to finish in the points. nother absentee was Ludwig so Ghinzani epped up a grade from C2 to be the new an for Taka-Q alongside the underrated arilla as Joest's famous number seven on joined those in contention for utright honours.

Warwick's chances then took a knock

when the car he was to share with Lammers suffered hub failure so the Englishman ousted Schlesser from alongside Cheever and the Silverstone winning pair set out after further glory. By half distance they were third behind Ghinzani/Barilla and Larrauri/Pareja, then second when the Brun car suffered brake problems. It was at this point that the Bell/ Stuck 962, weighed down by PDK and ABS, really started to accumulate its ill fortune. Then the gremlins, having feasted on the Porsche, obviously wanted to taste something different and transferred their attentions to the XJR-6 when, firstly, Warwick was called in to be reprimanded for ignoring instructions after taking to an escape road at the chicane, then Cheever lost a couple of minutes when the master switch was knocked off after hitting debris and, finally, the electronic goodies went bad inducing a misfire. All were easily resolved but time had been lost, time that would prove valuable come the setting sun.....

So just as it was at Spa, it was down to Warwick to chase a Brun Porsche although on this occasion there was the Taka-Q 956 ahead of them both en route to a marvellous victory for chassis 117 before its impending retirement. What a way to go!

The Jaguar managed to claw back two thirds of the deficit between it and its adversary over the last dozen laps, but was still nearly half a minute adrift when the flag came out. Several of the all important computer readouts indicated that the XJR-6 was in second spot and as one of these was the official scoreboard, Warwick was acclaimed as World Champion with the Silk Cut-TWR equipe heralded as winners of the team prize.

It was time for celebration - or was it? While the marketing men contemplated the headlines - the new XJ6 was being launched the following week - those on the

racing side of the liaison were not yet a-partying, even when Derek was handed the trophy at the prize-giving ceremony. Discussions ensued between interested parties and the organisers to check lap charts with the eventual conclusion, after two hours deliberation, that somehow, somewhere the Jaguar had been wrongly accredited with one more lap than it had actually achieved and thus deducted Warwick and Cheever WERE, as many suspected, only third behind the Jelinski/Dickens Brun 956.

This effectively transferred the Teams' title to the Swiss concern and the Drivers' to Bell and Stuck from whence it had come, leaving the Silk Cats clutching at straws. Excuse me, Warwick-san, can we have our cup back?

Not that it was the end of the matter for Team Manager Roger Silman, armed with all that experience TWR had gleaned from Group Aggravation saloons, promptly put in a protest, which was rejected, then an appeal which guaranteed that the matter would finally be adjudicated many months hence in far off Paris.

If C1 gave all the appearances of having the grace of a chimps tea party then C2 was a teddy bears' picnic for if the champagne was put on ice at Kidlington, then they were surely breaking out the saki and scotch at Salcey Forest, home of Ecurie Ecosse. Mallock and Duez again saw off all opposition to record their fourth consecutive class success after an almost faultless run while the troubled Fiero could not maintain its momentum for the race nor the title, nevertheless still finishing well clear of the pole winning Argo of Schanche and Kleppe. So it was that the Metro V6 claimed its first World Championship, a remarkable feat considering that a year ago it was destined more for Kielder than Copse. If you go down to the woods today....

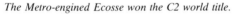
The Metro-engined Ecosse won the C2 world title.

DEREK BELL – World Champion again

Some weeks after Fuji it was announced by FISA that Derek Bell, and he alone, was World Champion - Hans Stuck was runner up! It had apparently escaped everyone's attention but in *les petits mots*, the small-print, or the gospel according to Jean-Marie, there were contingency plans in the event of a tie and unlike last season the Rothmans pairings had once, at Norising, split their efforts.

At the sprint race, Hanschen was, you will recall, highly competitive all weekend only to lose a quite probable victory due to a niggling problem with a PDK transmission which dropped him to 15th at the finish: all glory no garlands. Meanwhile Derek's venture in the JFR 956 had been fraught with handling and overheating dramas to

finish out of the points in 11th spot maintaining the status quo on his regular partner.

If the German organisers had not insisted on single driver entries the Bell/Stuck combination would have shared the car, shared the result, shared the title. It had been decreed.....

DIMENSIONS

Model	Length	Width	Height	Wheel Base	Front Track	Rear Track	Engine Type	C.C.	B.H.P.
Jaguar XJR-6	4800	2000	1028	2780	1500	1450	V-12	6500	630
Kouros C-8	4800	1980	1070	2780	1616	1550	V-8	5000T	650
Porsche 962C	4800	2000	1030	2770	1665	1545	F-6	2649T	630
Porsche 956	4800	2000	1030	2650	1665	1545	F-6	2649T	630
Toyota 86C-L	4650	1990	960	2600	1660	1570	S-4	2090T	503
Nissan R86V	4800	2000	1090	2670	1600	1550	V-6	3000T	700
Cougar C-12	4800	1990	1050	2680	1500	1520	F-6	2649T	630
WM P-82 (CI)	4120	1780	1020	2320	1470	1360	V-6	2850T	600
Porsche 961	4380	1890	1260	2310	1522	1580	F-6	2847T	680
Mazda 757	4550	1980	1010	2580	1570	1490	R-3	1962R	450
Spice SC86C	4510	1822	1029	2670	1480	1468	V-8	3300	550
Gebhardt 843	4600	2000	1003	2595	1644	1542	V-8	3300	550
Ecosse 286	4297	2000	*	2393	1394	1394	V-6	2991	410

Graham Gauld of the Ecosse team was unable to advise the overall height of their new Rover engined challenger but offered by way of guidance that it came "about half way up my zip fly". The mind boggles!

QUALIFICATIONS

No	Drivers	Marques	GR	1st Practice	2nd Practice	Time	Practice	Speed
2	Rothmans Porsche J. Mass, B. Wollek	Porsche 962C	C1	3'15.99	3'27.36	3'15.99	1	248.486
1	Rothmans Porsche D. Bell, H. J. Stuck, A. Holbert	Porsche 962C	C1	3'16.60	3'38.21	3'16.60	1	247.715
7	Joest Racing K. Ludwig, P. Barilla, J. Winter	Porsche 956	C1	3'17.11	3'25.79	3'17.11	1	247.074
19	Brun Motorsport T. Boutsen, D. Theys, A. Ferte	Porsche 956	C1	3'26.74	3'20.10	3'20.10	2	243.382
51	Silk Cut TWR Jaguar D. Warwick, E. Cheever, J. L. Schlesser	Jaguar XJR6	C1	3'21.60	3'25.59	3'21.60	1	241.571
17	Brun Motorsport O. Larrauri, J. Pareja, J. Gouhier	Porsche 962C	C1	3'30.70	3'23.47	3'23.47	2	239.351
52	Silk Cut TWR Jaguar B. Redman, H. Haywood, H. Heyer	Jaguar XJR6	C1	3'28.81	3'24.95	3'24.95	2	237.622
3	Rothmans Porsche V. Schuppan, D. Olson	Porsche 962C	C1	3'31.76	3'25.34	3'25.34	2	237.171
62	Kouros Racing H. Pescarolo, C. Danner, D. Quester	Kouros Mercedes	C1	3'34.96	3'26.69	3'26.69	2	235.622
13	Primagaz Y. Courage, A. de Cadenet, Raphanel	Cougar C12	C1	3'31.39	3'26.98	3'26.98	2	235.292
8	Joest Racing G. Follmer, J. Morton, K. Miller	Porsche 956	C1	3'27.37	3'27.72	3'27.37	1	234.849
18	Brun Motorsport W. Brun, M. Sigala, F. Jelinski	Porsche 962C	C1	3'28.22	3'28.05	3'28.05	2	234.082
61	Kouros Racing Nielsen, Thackwell, Pescarolo	Kouros Mercedes	C1	3'31.13	3'29.22	3'29.22	2	232.773
53	Silk Cut TWR Jaguar G. Brancatelli, W. Percy, A. Hahne	Jatuar XJR6	C1	3'29.25	3'29.24	3'29.24	2	232.750
10	Porsche Kremer Racing Gartner, Van Der Merwe, Takahashi	Porsche 962C	C1	3'31.17	3'30.10	3'30.10	2	231.798
14	L. M. Equipe M. Baldi, P. Cobb, R. Dyson	Porsche 956	C1	3'46.13	3'30.31	3'30.31	2	231.566
55	John Fitzpatrick Racing Alliot, Romero, Trolle, Konrad	Porsche 956	C1	3'48.66	3'33.86	3'33.86	2	227.722
41	Secateva J. D. Raulet, M. Pignard, F. Migault	WM	C1	3'33.97	3'34.86	3'33.97	1	227.605

QUALIFICATIONS (Continued)

	No	Drivers	Marques	GR	1st Practice	2nd Practice	Time	Practice	Speed
19.	9	Obermaier Racing GmbH J. Lassig, F. M. Ballabio, D. Wood	Porsche 956	C1	3'41.49	3'25.27	3'35.27	2	226.231
20.	33	Danone Porsche España E. De Villota, F. Velez, G. Fouche	Porsche 956	C1	3'37.75	3'35.99	3'35.99	2	225.477
21.	63	Ernst Schuster S. Brunn, E. Schuster, R. Seher	Porsche 936	C1	3'37.42	3'44.61	3'37.42	1	223.994
22.	12	Primagaz P. Yver, H. Striebig, Cohen Olivar	Porsche 956	C1	3'39.79	3'39.56	3'39.56	2	221.810
23.	70	Spice Engineering Ltd G. Spice, R. Bellm, J. M. Martin	Spice Pontiac Ford	C2	3'43.86	3'40.47	3'40.47	2	220.895
24.	199	Porsche Training	Porsche 962C	C1	3'40.85		3'40.85	1	220.515
25.	23	Nissan Motorsports Int. K. Hoshino, K. Matsumoto, A. Suzuki	Nissan R86V	C1	3'41.49	3'49.73	3'41.49	1	219.878
26.	171	Mazda Speed Co Ltd Y. Katayama, Y. Terada, T. Yorino	Mazda 757	GTP	3'43.31	3'45.90	3'43.31	1	218.086
27.	180	Porsche AG R. Metge, C. Ballot-Lena	Porsche 961	GTX	3'46.91	3'43.45	3'43.45	2	217.949
28.	102	L. Rossiaud N. Del Bello, L. Rossiaud, B. Sotty	Rondeau M379	C2	3'43.74	4'00.34	3'43.74	1	217.666
29.	74	Gebhardt Racing Cars De Thoisy, Dickens, Yvon	Gebhardt JC843	C2	3'46.50	3'44.57	3'44.57	2	216.862
30.	170	Mazda Speed Co Ltd D. Kennedy, M. Galvin, P. Dieudonne	Mazda 757	GTP	3'44.74	3'45.49	3'44.74	1	216.698
31.	38	Dome Co Ltd E. Elgh, B. Gabbiani, T. Suzuki	Dome Toyota B6C	C1	3'45.25	3'57.30	3'45.25	1	216.207
32.	47	Graff Racing Grand, Goudchaux, Menant	Rondeau M482	C1	3'49.59	3'47.17	3'47.17	2	214.380
33.	21	Richard Cleare Racing R. Cleare, L. Robert, G. Newsum	March Porsche	GTP	4'00.08	3'47.32	3'47.32	2	214.238
34.	32	Nissan Motorsports Int. M. Hasemi, T. Wada, J. Weaver	Nissan R85V	C1	3'55.01	3'47.35	3'47.35	2	214.210
35.	100	Secateva R. Dorchy, P. Pessiot, C. Haldi	WM P85	C2	3'48.55	3'54.18	3'48.55	1	213.085
36.	198		Mazda Training			3'48.77	3'48.77	2	212.881
37.	45	P. Oudet P. Oudet, J. C. Justice	Rondeau M382	C1	3'49.13		3'49.13	1	212.546
38.	95	R. Bassaler R. Bassaler, D. Lacaud, Y. Tapy	Sauber C6	C2	3'59.09	3'53.27	3'53.27	2	208.774
39.	89	Martin Schanche Racing M. Schanche, T. Kleppe, M. Birrane	Argo JM19	C2	4'15.15	3'53.49	3'53.49	2	208.577
40.	90	Jens Winther J. Winther, D. Mercer, L. Jensen	URD BMW	C2	3'58.98	3'53.85	3'53.85	2	208.256
41.	83	Luigi Taverna Taverna, Palma, Vanoli, Pallavicini	Alba AR3	C2	4'33.84	3'54.51	3'54.51	2	207.670
42.	36	Tom's Co Ltd S. Nakajima, G. Lees, M. Sekiya	Tom's Toyota B6C	C1	3'54.85		3'54.85	1	207.369
43.	79	Ecurie Ecosse R. Mallock, M. Wilds, D. Leslie	Ecosse C286	C2	3'55.35	4'20.27	3'55.35	1	206.929
44.	75	Ada Engineering I. Harrower, E. Clements, T. Dodd-Noble	Gebhardt JC843	C2	3'56.99	4'30.54	3'56.99	1	205.497
45.	99	Roy Baker Racing Tiga N. Nicholson, J. Sheldon, J. Thyrring	Tiga Ford GC86	C2	4'03.23	3'57.36	3'57.36	2	205.176
46.	92	Louis Descartes J. Heuclin, L. Descartes	ALD 02	C2	4'01.95	3'57.59	3'57.59	2	204.978
47.	66	Cosmik Racing Promotions C. Los, R. Touroul, P. Dermagne	March 84G	C1	4'05.30	3'59.21	3'59.21	2	203.590
48.	97	Roy Baker Racing Tiga E. Thomas, V. Musetti, M. Allison	Tiga Ford GC84	C2	4'57.61	3'59.60	3'59.60	2	203.258
49.	72	J. Bartlett/Goodmans R. Donovan, R. Jones, N. Adams	Bardon DB1	C2	4'06.77	3'59.97	3'59.97	2	202.943
50.	98	Roy Baker Racing Tiga M. Hall, D. Andrews, D. Bain	Tiga Ford GC86	C2	4'13.39	4'02.78	4'02.78	2	200.596
51.	78	Ecurie Ecosse L. Delano, A. Petery, J. Hotchkiss	Ecosse C285	C2	4'03.98	4'05.64	4'03.98	1	199.609
52.	111	MK Motorsport M. Krankenberg, P. Witmeur, J. Libert	BMW M1	SPDR	4'08.68	4'15.87	4'08.68	1	195.837
53.	20	Tiga Team T. L. Davey, Nn. Crang, J. Gimbel	Tiga	C1	4'51.41	4'09.58	4'09.58	2	195.131
54.	106	Strandell L. Hellberg, K. Leim, Fritsch	Strandell Porsche	C2	4'51.79	4'19.32	4'19.32	2	187.801

AT 10.00 pm SATURDAY

No.	Drivers	Marques	Hours	Laps	Kms	Average	Group
1	D. Bell, H. J. Stuck, A. Holbert	Porsche 962C	5h58'30.7	99	1339	224.138	C1
2	J. Mass, B. Wollek	Porsche 962C	5h59'27.9	99	1339	223.544	C1
7	K. Ludwig, P. Barilla, J. Winter	Porsche 956	5h59'45.8	99	1339	223.358	C1
51	D. Warwick, E. Cheever, J. L. Schlesser	Jaguar XJR6	5h54'46.2	97	1312	221.926	C1
53	G. Brancatelli, W. Percy, A. Hahne	Jaguar XJR6	5h57'25.0	96	1299	218.012	C1
17	Ol Larrauri, J. Pareja, J. Gouhier	Porsche 962C	5h59'53.2	96	1299	216.516	C1
10	Gartner, Van Der Merwe, Takahashi	Porsche 962C	5h54'46.8	93	1258	212.769	C1
33	E. De Villota, F. Velez, G. Fouche	Porsche 956	5h57'01.8	93	1258	211.428	C1
55	Alliot, Romero, Trolle	Porsche 936	5h56'37.1	91	1231	207.120	C1
63	S. Brunn, E. Schuster, R. Seher	Porsche 936	5h56'51.5	90	1218	204.706	C1
9	J. Lassig, F. M. Ballabio, D. Wood	Porsche 956	5h57'50.3	90	1218	204.145	C1
12	P. Yver, H. Striebig, Cohen Olivar	Porsche 956	5h58'31.5	90	1218	203.754	C1
8	G. Follmer, J. Morton, K. Miller	Porsche 956	5h58'47.1	90	1218	203.607	C1
19	T. Boutsen, D. Theys, A. Ferte	Porsche 956	5h37'35.1	89	1204	213.989	C1
170	D. Kennedy, M. Galvin, P. Dieudonne	Mazda 757	5h59'48.9	88	1190	198.512	GTP
32	M. Hasemi, T. Wada, J. Weaver	Nissan R 85 V	5h56'47.0	87	1177	197.924	C1
38	E. Elgh, B. Gabbiani, T. Suzuki	Dome Toyota 86C	5h57'07.5	87	1177	197.735	C1
36	S. Nakajima, G. Lees, M. Sekiya	Tom's Toyota 86C	5h58'32.6	87	1177	196.952	C1
41	J. D. Raulet, M. Pignard, F. Migault	WM	5h59'02.9	87	1177	196.675	C1
79	R. Mallock, M. Wilds, D. Leslie	Ecosse C286	5h53'14.6	86	1163	197.610	C2
45	P. Oudet, J. C. Justice	Rondeau M382	5h57'02.2	86	1163	195.510	C1
180	R. Metge, C. Ballot-Lena	Porsche 961	5h58'36.2	85	1150	192.393	GTX
21	R. Cleare, L. Robert, G. Newsum	March Porsche	5h59'48.5	85	1150	191.748	GTP
102	N. Del Bello, L. Rossiaud, B. Sotty	Rondeau M 379	5h59'36.7	84	1136	189.596	C2
78	L. Delano, A. Petery, J. Hotchkiss	Ecosse C285	5h57'20.8	83	1123	188.526	C2
90	J. Winther, D. Mercer, L. Jensen	URD	5h56'16.3	82	1109	186.817	C2
70	G. Spice, R. Bellm, J. M. Martin	Spice Pontiac Fiero	5h32'39.8	80	1082	195.195	C2
47	Grand, Goudchaux, Menant	Rondeau M482	5h56'20.2	80	1082	182.227	C1
111	M. Krankenberg, P. Witmeur, J. Libert	BMW M1	5h59'13.1	80	1082	180.765	SPOR
75	I. Harrower, E. Clements, T. Dodd-Noble	Gebhardt JC843	5h59'59.5	79	1069	178.122	C2
14	M. Baldi, P. Cobb, R. Dyson	Porsche 956	5h59'46.6	76	1028	171.461	C1
18	W. Brun, M. Sigala, F. Jelinski	Porsche 962C	4h45'08.0	75	1015	213.500	C1
62	H. Pescarolo, C. Danner, D. Quester	Kouros Mercedes	5h58'38.2	75	1015	169.742	C1
100	R. Dorchy, P. Pessiot, C. Haldi	WM P85	5h12'48.8	74	1001	192.013	C2
97	E. Thomas, V. Musetti, M. Allison	Tiga Ford GC84	5h58'32.1	74	1001	167.527	C2
66	C. Los, R. Touroul, N. Crang	March 84G	5h59'05.8	73	988	165.004	C1
99	N. Nicholson, J. Sheldon, J. Thyrring	Tiga Ford GC86	5h56'52.3	71	960	161.484	C2
95	R. Bassaler, D. Lacaud, Y. Tapy	Sauber C6	5h56'28.1	70	947	159.390	C2
74	De Thoisy, Dickens, Yvon	Gebhardt JC843	5h02'56.3	68	920	182.196	C2
83	Taverna, Palma, Vanoli	Alba AR3	5h57'37.1	65	879	147.529	C2
23	K. Hoshino, K. Matsumoto, A. Suzuki	Nissan R86V	4h18'08.8	64	866	201.232	C1
61	Nielsen, Thackwell, Pescarolo	Kouros Mercedes	4h43'55.5	61	825	174.385	C1
171	Y. Katayama, Y. Terada, T. Yorino	Mazda 757	3h54'49.9	59	798	203.929	GTP
72	R. Donovan, R. Jones, N. Adams	Bardon DB1	5h40'14.6	55	744	131.207	C2
52	B. Redman, H. Haywood, H. Heyer	Jaguar XJR6	3h13'39.0	53	717	222.148	C1
92	J. Heuclin, L. Descartes	ALD 02	4h27'51.9	41	555	124.237	C2
13	Y. Courage, A. De Cadenet, Raphanel	Cougar C12	5h57'57.6	24	325	54.420	C1

	Best lap						
7	K. Ludwig, P. Barilla, J. Winter	Porsche 956	3'23.3	71		239.551	

	Retired						
89	M. Schanche, T. Kleppe, M. Birrane	Argo JM19	5'58.9	1		14	
98	M. Hall, D. Andrews, D. Bain	Tiga Gord GC86	5'14.5	1	14		
3	V. Schuppan, D. Olson	Porsche 962C	2h32'35.4	41		555	

AT 4.00 am SUNDAY

	No.	Drivers	Marques	Hours	Laps	Kms	Average	Group
1.	7	K. Ludwig, P. Barilla, J. Winter	Porsche 956	11h52'26.2	191	2584	217.606	C1
2.	1	D. Bell, H. J. Stuck, A. Holbert	Porsche 962C	11h52'29.4	191	2584	217.590	C1
3.	17	O. Larrauri, J. Pareja, J. Gouhier	Porsche 962C	11h55'46.8	183	2476	207.518	C1
4.	51	D. Warwick, E. Cheever, J. L. Schlesser	Jaguar XJR6	11h55'40.9	182	2462	206.412	C1
5.	33	E. De Villota, F. Velez, G. Fouche	Porsche 956	11h52'24.0	180	2435	205.084	C1
6.	8	G. Follmer, J. Morton, K. Miller	Porsche 956	11h52'31.2	178	2408	202.771	C1
7.	9	J. Lassig, F. M. Ballabio, D. Wood	Porsche 956	11h55'37.1	175	2367	198.491	C1
8.	63	S. Brunn, E. Schuster, R. Seher	Porsche 936	11h52'36.4	173	2340	197.052	C1
9.	55	Alliot, Romero, Trolle	Porsche 956	11h37'51.0	170	2300	197.729	C1
10.	38	E. Elgh, B. Gabbiani, T. Suzuki	Dome Toyota 86C	11h55'39.8	168	2273	190.539	C1
11.	180	R. Metge, C. Ballot-Lena	Porsche 961	11h55'26.0	167	2259	189.466	GTX
12.	32	M. Hasemi, T. Wada, J. Weaver	Nissan R 85 V	11h55'42.2	165	2232	187.126	C1
13.	12	P. Yver, H. Striebig, Cohen Olivar	Porsche 956	11h29'15.1	160	2164	188.420	C1
14.	79	R. Mallock, M. Wilds, D. Leslie	Ecosse C286	11h05'08.9	159	2151	194.027	C2
15.	75	I. Harrower, E. Clements, T. Dodd	Gebhardt JC843	11h52'38.0	158	2137	179.959	C2
16.	47	Grand, Goudchaux, Menant	Rondeau M482	11h52'25.0	156	2110	177.735	C1
17.	90	J. Winther, D. Mercer, L. Jensen	URD	11h55'33.3	156	2110	176.956	C2
18.	111	M. Krankenberg, P. Witmeur, J. Libert	BMW M1	11h55'31.8	151	2043	171.290	SPOR
19.	14	M. Baldi, P. Cobb, R. Dyson	Porsche 956	11h55'51.6	150	2029	170.077	C1
20.	66	C. Los, R. Tourdul, N. Crang	March 846	11h55'30.9	148	2002	167.891	C1
21.	100	R. Dorchy, P. Pessiot, C. Haldi	WM P85	11h55'29.8	144	1948	163.357	C2
22.	21	R. Cleare, L. Robert, G. Newsum	March Porsche	11h52'34.1	142	1921	161.750	GTP
23.	102	N. Del Bello, L. Rossiaud, B. Sotty	Rondeau M 379	11h55'39.5	139	1880	157.649	C2
24.	78	L. Delano, A. Petery, J. Hotchkiss	Ecosse C285	11h55'51.1	139	1880	157.607	C2
25.	95	R. Bassaler, D. Lacaud, Y. Tapy	Sauber Co	11h52'28.6	128	1732	145.822	C2
26.	70	G. Spice, R. Bellm, J. M. Martin	Spice Pontiac Fiero	11h55'53.8	128	1732	145.125	C2
27.	99	N. Nicholson, J. Sheldon, J. Thyrring	Tiga Ford GC86	11h52'32.9	112	1515	127.581	C2
28.	72	R. Donovan, R. Jones, N. Adams	Bardon DB1	11h55'27.0	110	1488	124.795	C2
29.	13	Y. Courage, A. De Cadenet, Raphanel	Cougar C12	11h55'48.1	105	1420	119.064	C1
30.	97	E. Thomas, V. Musetti, M. Allison	Tiga Ford GC84	7h57'08.4	95	1285	161.607	C2

| | **Best lap** | | | | | | | |
| | 7 | K. Ludwig, P. Barilla, J. Winter | Porsche 956 | 3'23.3 | 71 | | 239.551 | |

	Retired							
	89	M. Schanche, T. Kleppe, M. Birrane	Argo JM19	0h05'58.9	1	14		
	98	M. Hall, D. Andrews, D. Bain	Tiga Ford GC86	0h05'14,5	1	14		
	92	J. Heuclin, L. Descartes	ALD 02	4h27'51.9	41	555		
	3	V. Schuppan, D. Olson	Porsche 962 C	2h32'35.4	41	555		
	52	B. Redman, H. Haywood, H. Heyer	Jaguar XJR6	3h13'39.0	53	717		
	171	Y. Katayama, Y. Terada, T. Yorino	Mazda 757	3h54'49.9	59	798		
	61	Nielsen, Thackwell, Pescarolo	Kouros Mercedes	4h43'55.5	61	825		
	23	K. Hoshino, K. Matsumoto, A. Suzuki	Nissan R86V	4h18'08.8	64	866		
	74	De Thoisy, Dickens, Yvon	Gebhardt JC843	5h02'56.3	68	920		
	83	Taverna, Palma, Vanoli	Alba AR3	6h42'10.6	74	1001		
	18	W. Brun, M. Sigala, F. Jelinski	Porsche 962C	4h45'08.0	75	1015		
	62	H. Pescarolo, C. Danner, D. Quester	Kouros Mercedes	6h41'29.8	86	1163		
	19	T. Boutsen, D. Theys, A. Ferte	Porsche 956	5h37'35.1	89	12.04		
	36	S. Nakajima, G. Lees, M. Sekiya	Tom's Toyota 86C	7h28'51.6	105	1420		
	45	P. Oudet, J. C. Justice	Rondeau M382	8h35'29.9	110	1488		
	41	J. D. Raulet, M. Pignard, F. Migault	WM	9h17'05.0	132	1786		
	170	D. Kennedy, M. Galvin, P. Dieudonne	Mazda 757	9h42'08.9	137	1853		
	53	G. Brancatelli, W. Percy, A. Hahne	Jaguar XJR6	9h41'45.7	154	2083		
	10	Gartner, Van Der Merwe, Takahashi	Porsche 962 C	11h12'20.6	169	2286		
	2	J. Mass, B. Wollek, V. Schuppan	Porsche 962 C	11h00'02.5	180	2435		

AT 10.00 am SUNDAY

	No.	Drivers	Marques	Hours	Laps	Kms	Average	Group
.	1	D. Bell, H. J. Stuck, A. Holbert	Porsche 962 C	17h59'37.6	273	3693	205.245	C1
.	17	O. Larrauri, J. Pareja, J. Gouhier	Porsche 962 C	17h58'28.3	264	3571	198.691	C1
.	8	G. Follmer, J. Morton, K. Miller	Porsche 956	17h56'08.6	259	3504	193.350	C1
.	33	E. De Villota, F. Velez, G. Fouche	Porsche 956	17h56'34.1	259	3504	195.273	C1
.	9	J. Lassig, F. M. Ballabio, D. Wood	Porsche 956	17h59'54.1	252	3409	189.409	C1
.	63	S. Brunn, E. Schuster, R. Seher	Porsche 936	17h56'17.7	251	3396	189.289	C1
.	38	E. Elgh, B. Gabbiani, T. Suzuki	Dome Toyota 86C	17h57'31.5	240	3247	180.787	C1
.	55	Alliot, Romero, Trolle	Porsche 956	17h57'13.7	237	3206	178.576	C1
.	55	M. Hasemi, T. Wada, J. Weaver	Nissan R 85 V	17h52'54.8	236	3193	178.538	C1
.	75	I. Harrower, E. Clements, T. Dodd-Noble	Gebhart JC843	17h56'46.4	232	3138	174.883	C2
.	180	R. Metge, C. Ballot-Lena	Porsche 961	17h57'02.1	231	3125	174.087	GTX
.	47	Grand, Goudchaux, Menant	Rondeau M482	17h56'25.5	227	3071	171.169	C1
.	90	J. Winther, D. Mercer, L. Jensen	URD	17h54'21.7	226	3057	170.742	C2
.	14	M. Baldi, P. Cobb, R. Dyson	Porsche 956	17h59'03.5	224	3030	168.495	C1
.	21	R. Cleare, L. Robert, G. Newsum	March Porsche	17h58'49.6	218	2949	164.017	GTP
.	100	R. Dorschy, P. Pessiot, C. Haldi	WM P85	17h59'50.7	217	2936	163.110	C2
.	111	M. Krankenberg, P. Witmeur, J. Libert	BMW M1	17h58'23.6	212	2868	159.567	SPOR
.	78	L. Delano, A. Petery, J. Hotchkiss	Ecosse C285	17h56'52.0	211	2854	159.039	C2
.	102	N. Del Bello, L. Rossiaud, B. Sotty	Rondeau M 379	17h57'38.7	194	2624	146.120	C2
.	70	G. Spice, R. Bellm, J. M. Martin	Spice Pontiac Fiero	17h57'40.4	182	2462	137.078	C2
.	95	R. Bassaler, D. Lacaud, Y. Tapy	Sauber C6	16h22'15.9	177	2394	146.261	C2
.	13	Y. Courage, A. De Cadenet, Raphanel	Cougar C12	17h50'12.1	176	2381	133.484	C1
.	72	R. Donovan, R. Jones, N. Adams	Bardon DB1	17h59'03.8	175	2367	131.636	C2
.	99	N. Nicholson, J. Sheldon, J. Thyrring	Tiga Ford GC86	14h23'30.7	125	1691	117.494	C2

Best lap								
	7	K. Ludwig, P. Barilla, J. Winter	Porsche 956	3'23.3	71		239.551	

Retired								
	89	M. Schanche, T. Kleppe, M. Birrane	Argo JM19	0h05'58.9	1	14		
	98	M. Hall, D. Andrews, D. Bain	Tiga Ford GC86	0h05'14.5	1	14		
	92	J. Heuclin, L. Descartes	ALD 02	4h27'51.9	41	555		
	3	V. Schuppan, D. Olson	Porsche 962 C	2h32'35.4	41	555		
	52	B. Redman, H. Haywood, H. Heyer	Jaguar XJR6	3h13'39.0	53	717		
	171	Y. Katayama, Y. Terada, T. Yorino	Mazda 757	3h54'49.9	59	798		
	61	Nielsen, Thackwell, Pescarolo	Kouros Mercedes	4h43'55.5	61	825		
	23	K. Hoshino, K. Matsumoto, A. Suzuki	Nissan R86V	4h18'08.8	64	866		
	74	De Thoisy, Dickens, Yvon	Gebhardt JC843	5h02'56.3	68	920		
	83	Taverna, Palma, Vanoli	Alba AR3	6h42'10.6	74	1001		
	18	W. Brun, M. Sigala, F. Jelinski	Porsche 962C	4h45'08.0	75	1015		
	62	H. Pescarolo, C. Danner, D. Quester	Kouros Mercedes	6h41'29.8	86	1163		
	19	T. Bousten, D. Theys, A. Ferte	Porsche 956	5h37'35.1	89	1204		
	97	E. Thomas, V. Musetti, M. Allison	Tiga Ford GC84	7h57'08.4	95	1285		
	36	S. Nakajima, G. Lees, M. Sekiya	Tom's Toyota 86C	7h28'51.6	105	1420		
	45	P. Oudet, J. C. Justice	Rondeau M382	8h35'29.9	110	1488		
	41	J. D. Raulet, M. Pignard, F. Migault	WM	9h17'05.0	132	1786		
	170	D. Kennedy, M. Galvin, P. Dieudonne	Mazda 757	9h42'08.9	137	1853		
	53	G. Brancatelli, W. Percy, A. Hahne	Jaguar XJR6	9h41'45.7	154	2083		
	12	P. Yver, H. Striebig, Cohen Olivar	Porsche 956	11h29'15.1	160	2164		
	66	C. Loss, R. Tourol, N. Crang	March 84G	15h00'48.3	169	2286		
	10	Gartner, Van Der Merne, Takahashi	Porsche 962 C	11h12'20.6	169	2286		
	2	J. Mass, B. Wollek, V. Schuppan	Porsche 962 C	11h00'02.5	180	2435		
	79	R. Mallock, M. Wilds, D. Leslie	Ecosse C286	15h28'39.2	181	2449		
	7	K. Ludwig, P. Barilla, J. Winter	Porsche 956	12h29'09.5	196	2651		

54th LE MANS 24 HOURS (F)

Pos	Drivers(Nat)	Team/Sponsor	No	Class	Car-Engine	Tyres	Result	Weight(kgs)	Speed(mph)
1	Hans Joachim Stuck (D) Derek Bell (GB) Al Holbert (USA)	Works/Rothmans	1	C1	2.6t Porsche 962-003	D	367 laps	886	224
2	Oscar Larrauri (RA) Joël Gouhier (F) Jesus Pareja (E)	Brun/Fortuna	17	C1	2.6t Porsche 962-115	M	359 laps	905	207
3	George Follmer (USA) John Morton (USA) Kemper Miller (USA)	Joest/Gildred	8	C1	2.6t Porsche 956-104	G	354 laps	864	220
4	Emilio de Villota (E) George Fouche (ZA) Fermin Velez (E)	JFR/Danone	33	C1	2.6t Porsche 056-114	G	348 laps	882	204
5	Jurgen Laessig (D) Fulvio Ballabio (I) Dudley Wood (GB)	Obermaier/Topolino	9	C1	2.6t Porsche 956-109	G	344 laps	879	189
6	Siggi Brunn (D) Ernst Schuster (D) Ruedi Seher (D)	Schuster/McGregors	63	C1	2.8t Porsche 936CJ	D	343 laps	916	212
7	René Metge (F) Claude Ballot-Lena (F)	Works	180	GTX	2.6t Porsche 961	D	320 laps	1169	207
8	Evan Clements (GB) Ian Harrower (GB) Tom Dodd-Noble (GB)	ADA/Wang	75	C1	3.3 Gebhardt-Cosworth 843	A	317 laps	740	184
9	Mauro Baldi (I) Price Cobb (USA) Rob Dyson (USA)	RLR/Liqui-Moly	14	C1	2.6t Porsche 956-106B	G	317 laps	875	194
10	Philippe Alliot (F(Michel Trollé (F(Paco Romero (E)	JFR/Elkron &c	55	C1	2.6t Porsche 956-102/962c	G	311 laps	896	200
11	David Mercer (GB) Jens Winther (DK) Lars Givvo (DK)	Winther/Castrol	90	C2	3.5 URD-BMW C-82	A	309 laps	860	192
12	Claude Haldi (CH) Roger Dorchy (F) Pascal Pessiot (F)	Secateva	100	C2	2.6t WM Peugeot P-84	M	300 laps	826	203
13	Marc Menant (F) Jean-Philippe Grand (F) Jacques Goudchaux (F)	Graff/Ladubay	47	C1	3.3 Rondeau-Cosworth 482	G	298 laps	895	190
14	Lionel Robert (F) Richard Cleare (GB) Jack Newsum (USA)	Cleare/Bojolly's	21	GTP	2.8t March-Porsche 85-G	G	298 laps	942	174
15	Les Delano (USA) Andy Petery (USA) John Hotchkiss (USA)	Ecurie Ecosse	78	C2	3.3 Ecosse-Cosworth C-285	A	292 laps	795	182
16	James Weaver (GB) Masahiro Hasemi (J) Takao Wada (J)	Nismos/Amada	32	C1	3.0t March-Nissan 85-G	D	284 laps	972	202
17	Noël del Bello (F) Bruno Sotty (F) Lucien Rossiaud (F)	Rossiaud/Locatopp	102	C2	3.0 Rondeau-Cosworth 379	A	277 laps	778	203
18	Pierre-Henri Raphanel (F) Alain de Cadenet (GB) Yves Courage (F)	Works/Primagaz	13	C1	2.6t Cougar-Porsche C-12	M	266 laps	884	217
19	Ray Bellm (GB) Gordon Spice (GB) Jean-Michel Martin (B)	Spice/Listerine &C	70	C2	3.3 Spice-Cosworth SC-86C	A	257 laps	779	202
R	Eje Elgh (S) Beppe Gabbiani (I(Toshio Suzuki (J)	Dome/Formula	38	C1	2.1t Dome-Toyota 86-C	D	295 laps—turbo fire	894	188
NC	Pascal Witneur (B) Jean-Paul Libert (B) Michael Krankenbrug (D)	MK Motorsport	111	B	3.5 BMW M1	D	264 laps	1120	182
R	Derek Warwick (GB) Eddie Cheever (USA) Jean-Louis Schlesser (F)	TWR/Silk Cut	51	C1	6.0 Jaguar XJR6-286	D	239 laps—body damage	871	212
NC	Nick Adams (GB) Robin Donovan (GB) Richard Jones (GB)	Bartlett/Goodmans	72	C2	3.3 Bardon-Cosworth DB1	A	210 laps	809	159
NC	Dominique Lacaud (F) Yvon Tapy (F) Roland Bassaler (F)	Bassaler	95	C2	3.5 Sauber-BMW C-6	A	200 laps	866	180
R	Klaus Ludwig (D) Paolo Barilla (I) 'John Winter' (D)	Joest/Taka-Q	7	C1	2.6t Porsche 956-117	G	196 laps—engine	883	232
R	David Leslie (GB) Ray Mallock (GB) Mike Wilds (GB)	Ecurie Ecosse	79	C2	3.0 Ecosse-Rover C-286	A	181 laps—overheating	735	181
R	Bob Wollek (F) Jochen Mass (D) Vern Schuppan (AUS)	Works/Rothmans	2	C1	2.6t Porsche 962-004	D	180 laps—accident	879	218
R	Jo Gartner (A) Sarel van der Merwe (ZA) Kunimitsu Takahashi (J)	Kremer/Kenwood	10	C1	2.6t Porsche 962-118	Y	169 laps—accident	873	208
R	Costas Los (GR) Neil Crang (AUS) Raymond Touroul (F)	Cosmik/Metaxa	66	C1	2.6t March-Porsche 84-G	A	169 laps—electrics	924	188
R	Hubert Striebig (F) Pierre Yver (F) Max Olivar (MOR)	Kremer/Primagaz	12	C1	2.6t Porsche 956-105	Y	160 laps—withdrawn	874	218
R	Gianfranco Brancatelli (I) Win Percy (GB) Armin Hahne (D)	TWR/Silk Cut	53	C1	6.0 Jaguar XJR-385	D	154 laps—driveshaft	867	218
R	David Kennedy (IRL) Mark Galvin (IRL) Pierre Dieudonné (B)	Works/Lucky Strike	170	GTP	1.3r Mazda 757	D	137 laps—transmission	871	193
R	François Migault (F) Jean-Daniel Raulet (F) Michel Pignard (F)	Secateva/Vortice	41	C1	2.8t WM-Peugeot P-82	M	132 laps—engine	851	230
R	Nick Nicholson (USA) Thorkild Thyrring (DK) John Sheldon (GB)	RB Racing	99	C2	1.7t Tiga-Ford GC-285	D	125 laps—engine	756	182
R	Jean-Claude Justice (F) Patrick Oudet (F)	Oudet	45	C1	3.3 Rondeau-Cosworth 382	D	110 laps—oil pressure	899	185
R	Geoff Lees (GB) Satoru Nakajima (J) Masanori Sekiya (J)	Tom's/Leyton House	36	C1	2.1t Dome-Toyota 86-C	B	105 laps—engine	886	181
R	Mike Allison (USA) Val Musetti (GB) Tom Frank (USA)	RB Racing/Lucas	97	C2	1.7t Tiga-Ford GC-286	D	95 laps—electrics	779	—
R	Thierry Boutsen (B) Alain Ferté (F) Didier Theys (B)	Brun/Locatop	19	Cq	2.6t Porsche 962-106	M	89 laps—accident	907	202
R	Henri Pescarolo (F) Christian Danner (D) Dieter Quester (A)	Works/Kouros	62	C1	5.0 Sauber-Mercedes C-8	G	86 laps—transmission	886	207
R	Massimo Sigala (I) Walter Brun (CH) Frank Jelinski (D)	Brun/Torno	18	C1	2.6t Porsche 962-117	M	75 laps—engine	887	198
R	Luigi Taverna (I) Toni Palma (I) Marco Vanoli (CH)	Taverna	83	C2	3.3 Alba-Cosworth AR-3	A	74 laps—driveshaft	775	158
R	Stanley Dickens (S) Pierre de Thoisy (F) Jean-François Yvon (F)	Works/Rexona	74	C1	3.3 Gebhardt-Cosworth 853	A	68 laps—accident	801	190
R	Kazuyoshi Hoshino (J) Keiji Matsumoto (J) Aguri Suzuki (J)	Nismos/Amada	23	C1	3.0t March-Nissan 86-S	B	64 laps—engine	871	191
R	John Nielsen (DK) Mike Thackwell (NZ)	Works/Lucky Strike	61	C1	5.0t Sauber-Mercedes C-8	G	61 laps—engine	881	205
R	Takashi Yorino (J) Yojiro Katayama (J) Yojiro Terada (J)	Works/Lucky Strike	171	GTP	1.3r Mazda 757	D	59 laps—transmission	811	191
R	Hans Heyer (D) Brian Redman (GB) Hurley Haywood (USA)	TWR/Silk Cut	52	C1	6.0 Jaguar XJR-186	D	53 laps—fuel pressure	869	221
R	Vern Schuppan (AUS) Drake Olson (USA)	Works/Rothmans	3	C1	2.6t Porsche 962-002	D	41 laps—transmission	920	210
R	Jacques Heuclin (F) Louis Descartes (F)	Descartes/B&P	92	C2	3.5 ALD-BMW 02	A	41 laps—accident	736	180
R	David Andrews (GB) Mike Hall (AUS) Duncan Bain (GB)	RB Racing/Lucas	98	C2	1.7t Tiga-Ford GC-286	A	1 lap—driveshafts	779	183
R	Martin Birrane (IRL) Martin Schanche (N) Torgyer Kleppe (N)	MSR/Lucky Strike	89	C2	1.8t Argo-Zakspeed JM-19	G	1lap—engine	845	187
NQ	Neil Crang (AUS) Tim Lee-Davey (GB) John Gimbel (USA)	Tiga Team/Penthouse	20	C1	3.3t Tiga-Cosworth GC-85	D	NS—engine	899	—
NQ	Kenneth Leim (S) Peter Fritsch (D)	Strandell	106	C2	3.0 Strandell-Porsche	A	NS—fuel pressure	831	—

Winning distance: 3089.91 miles (4972.73 kms). **Average speed:** 128.75mph (207.197kmh). **Group C2:** 2668.93 miles, 111.21mph. **IMSA GTX:** 2694.25 miles, 112.26mph. Drivers in italics set qualifying times. First-named drivers started race. Car no 8 practised by Barilla and qualified by Ludwig. Car no 55 also driven in race by Haywood. Car no 55 qualified by Franz Konrad (D), did not race. Car no 66 also practised by Philippe Dermagne (F), did not race.

110

FASTEST LAPS

No	Drivers	Marques	Time	Lap	Speed	Hour	Group
7	K. Ludwig, P. Barilla, J. Winter	Porsche 956	3'23.3	71	239.551	4h16'27.9	C1
1	D. Bell, H. J. Stuck, A. Holbert	Porsche 962 C	3'23.7	7	239.081	0h24'02.8	C1
2	J. Mass, B. Wollek	Porsche 962 C	3'25.0	27	237.564	1h35.32.0	C1
52	B. Redman, H. Haywood, H. Heyer	Jaguar XJR6	3'25.8	53	236.641	3h13'39.0	C1
61	Nielsen, Thackwell, Pescarolo	Kouros Mercedes	3'26.3	39	236.067	3h19'55.1	C1
51	D. Warwick, E. Cheever, Jl. Schlesser	Jaguar XJR6	3'26.7	2	235.611	0h06'56.0	C1
3	V. Schuppan, D. Olson	Porsche 962 C	3'26.7	4	235.611	0h13'54.0	C1
19	T. Boutsen, D. Theys, A. Ferte	Porsche 956	3'27.0	3	235.269	0h10'26.7	C1
53	G. Brancatelli, W. Percy, A. Hahne	Jaguar XJR6	3'27.7	67	234.476	4h06'04.6	C1
10	Gartner, Van Der Merwe, Takahashi	Porsche 962 C	3'27.8	64	234.363	4h06'03.4	C1
17	O. Larrauri, J. Pareja, J. Gouhier	Porsche 962 C	3'27.9	3	234.251	0h10'31.5	C1
62	H. Pescarolo, C. Danner, D. Quester	Kouros Mercedes	3'28.7	29	233.353	3h04'10.8	C1
14	M. Baldi, P. Cobb, R. Dyson	Porsche 956	3'29.1	2	232.906	0h07'08.6	C1
8	G. Follmer, J. Morton, K. Miller	Porsche 956	3'31.8	2	229.937	0h07'10.8	C1
18	W. Brun, M. Sigala, F. Jelinski	Porsche 962 C	3'33.7	3	227.893	0h10'54.4	C1
9	J. Lassig, F. M. Ballabio, D. Wood	Porsche 956	3'36.1	4	225.362	0h14'34.1	C1
33	E. De Villota, F. Velez, G. Fouche	Porsche 956	3'36.4	66	225.049	4h11'53.1	C1
41	J. D. Raulet, M. Pignard, F. Migault	WM	3'36.5	4	224.945	0h14'42.5	C1
63	S. Brunn, E. Schuster, R. Seher	Porsche 936	3'36.9	4	224.531	0h14'40.5	C1
55	Alliot, Romero, Trolle	Porsche 956	3'36.9	63	224.531	4h05'13.2	C1
12	P. Yver, H. Striebig, Cohen Olivar	Porsche 956	3'37.3	44	224.117	2h53'45.0	C1
170	D. Kennedy, M. Galvin, P. Dieudonne	Mazda 757	3'40.9	47	220.465	3h09'23.9	GTP
23	K. Hoshino, K. Matsumoto, A. Suzuki	Nissan R86V	3'41.3	53	220.066	3h33'10.5	C1
32	M. Hasemi, T. Wada, J. Weaver	Nissan R 85 V	3'42.2	40	219.175	2h45'19.7	C1
38	E. Elgh, B. Gabbiani, T. Suzuki	Dome Toyota 86C	3'43.4	44	217.998	2h56'33.7	C1
13	Y. Courage, A. De Cadenet, Raphanel	Cougar C12	3'43.5	3	217.900	0h31'08.4	C1
70	G. Spice, R. Bellm, J. M. Martin	Spice Pontiac Fiero	3'43.7	3	217.705	0h11'36.6	C2
171	Y. Katayama, Y. Terada, T. Yorino	Mazda 757	3'45.9	24	215.585	1h34'17.2	GTP
74	De Thoisy, Dickens, Yvon	Gebhardt JC843	3'45.2	3	215.299	0h11'38.3	C2
21	R. Cleare, L. Robert, G. Newsum	March Porsche	3'46.5	52	215.014	3h41'35.3	GTP
45	P. Oudet, J. C. Justice	Rondeau M382	3'47.9	62	213.693	4h20'14.1	C1
180	R. Metge, C. Ballot-Lena	Porsche 961	3'48.1	63	213.506	4h17'42.5	GTX
100	R. Dorchy, P. Pessiot, C. Haldi	WM P85	3'50.1	2	211.650	0h08'27.5	C2
47	Grand, Goudchaux, Menant	Rondeau M482	3'51.0	20	210.825	1h35'14.3	C1
102	N. Del Bello, L. Rossiaud, B. Sotty	Rondeau M 379	3'51.1	38	210.734	2h36'32.6	C2
36	S. Nakajima, G. Lees, M. Sekiya	Tom's Toyota 86C	3'51.2	20	210.643	1h21'20.7	C1
66	C. Los, R. Touroul, N. Crang	March 84G	3'51.7	53	210.189	3h45'59.7	C1
75	I. Harrower, E. Clments, T. Dodd-Noble	Gebhardt JC843	3'53.7	39	208.390	2h57'26.2	C2
83	Taverna, Palma, Vanoli	Alba AR3	3'54.1	24	208.034	2h15'08.1	C2
79	R. Mallock, M. Wilds, D. Leslie	Ecosse C286	3'54.5	45	207.679	3h04'40.4	C2
99	N. Nicholson, J. Sheldon, J. Thyrring	Tiga Ford GC86	3'55.9	29	206.446	2h31'27.1	C2
90	J. Winther, D. Mercer, L. Jensen	U R D	3'56.4	18	206.010	1h15'28.3	C2
78	L. Delano, A. Petery, J. Hotchkiss	Ecosse C285	3'57.8	41	204.797	2h54'28.6	C2
97	E. Thomas, V. Musetti, M. Allison	Tiga Ford GC84	4'01.9	31	201.326	2h28'58.4	C2
95	R. Bassaler, D. Lacaud, Y. Tapy	Sauber C6	4'04.5	6	199.185	0h43'15.4	C2
92	J. Heuclin, L. Descartes	ALD 02	4'05.2	32	198.616	2h29'25.6	C2
111	M. Krankenberg, P. Witmeur, J. Libert	BMW M1	4'09.2	3	195.428	0h13'38.9	SPOR
72	R. Donovan, R. Jones, N. Adams	Bardon DB1	4'10.6	54	194.336	4h20'28.5	C2
98	M. Hall, D. Andrews, D. Bain	Tiga Ford GC86	5'14.5	1	154.851	0h05'14.5	C2
89	M. Schanche, T. Kleppe, M. Birrane	Argo JM19	5'58.9	1	135.694	0h05'58.9	C2